About this workbook

This book contains questions to target every topic in Year 3 English.

- Questions split into three levels of increasing difficulty – Challenge 1, Challenge 2 and Challenge 3 – to aid progress.
- Handy tips included.
- 'How am I doing?' checks for self-evaluation.
- Total marks boxes for each topic. 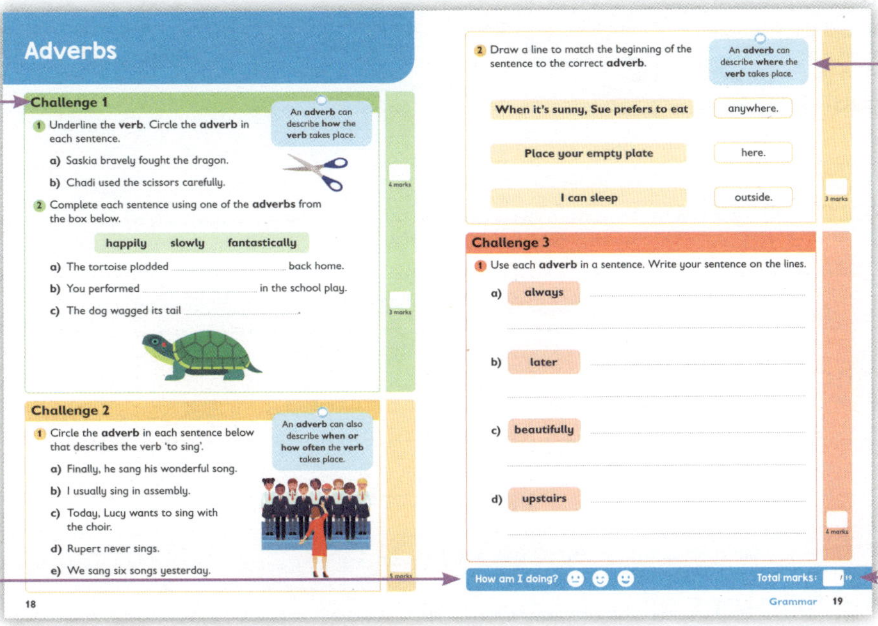
- Starter test recaps skills covered in Years 1 and 2.
- Four progress tests allow children to test how well they have remembered the information.
- QR codes link to online interactive quizzes for extra practice.
- Progress test charts to record results and identify which areas need further practice. 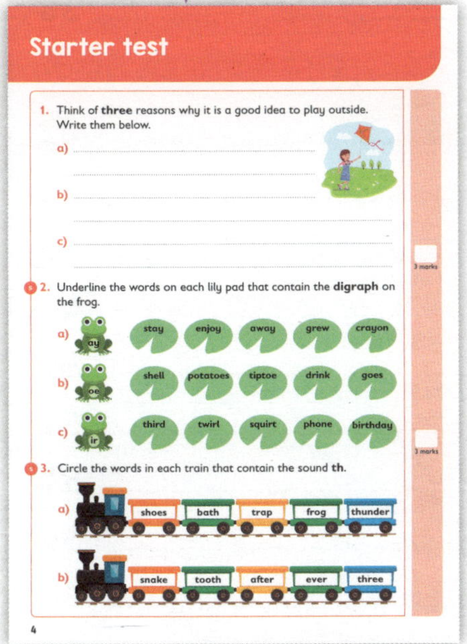 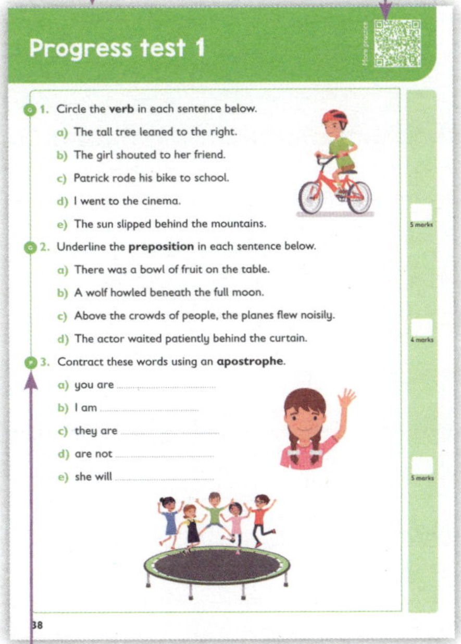 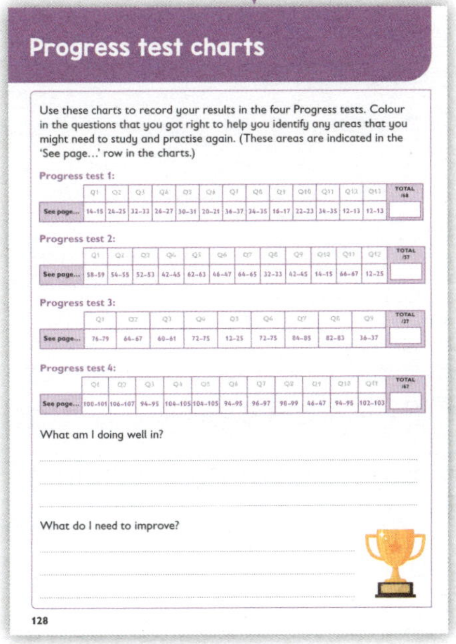
- Symbols to highlight questions that test grammar, punctuation and spelling in the starter test and progress tests.
- Answers are included at the back of the book.

Author: Sasha Wigley

Contents

Starter test 4

Grammar
Nouns and pronouns 12
Verbs 14
Present perfect form of verbs 16
Adverbs 18
Conjunctions 20
Conjunctions to show time (when) 22
Prepositions 24
Determiners 26

Punctuation
Capital letters and full stops 28
Commas for lists 30
Apostrophes for contractions 32
Possessive apostrophes 34
Using inverted commas for direct speech 36

Progress test 1 38

Spelling
Prefixes 1 42
Prefixes 2 44
Suffixes 1 46
Suffixes 2 48
Root words 50
Exception words 52
Etymology – the origin of words 54
Morphology – the formation of words 56
Homophones 58
Common misspellings 60
Vowels and consonants 62
Dictionaries 1 64
Dictionaries 2 66

Progress test 2 68

Contents

Reading – Comprehension

Fact retrieval 1	72
Fact retrieval 2	74
Traditional tales 1	76
Traditional tales 2	78
Poetry	80
Writer's purpose	82
Making predictions	84
Inference 1	86
Inference 2	88
Progress test 3	90

Writing – Composition

Learning from other writers	94
Sentence structure	96
Fronted adverbials	98
Organising non-fiction writing	100
Organising fiction writing	102
Character and setting description	104
Proofreading	106
Progress test 4	108
Answers	112
Progress test charts	128

ACKNOWLEDGEMENTS

The author and publisher are grateful to the copyright holders for permission to use quoted materials and images.

All illustrations and images are © Shutterstock.com and © HarperCollins*Publishers*

Every effort has been made to trace copyright holders and obtain their permission for the use of copyright material. The author and publisher will gladly receive information enabling them to rectify any error or omission in subsequent editions. All facts are correct at time of going to press.

Without limiting the exclusive rights of any author, contributor or the publisher, any unauthorised use of this publication to train generative artificial intelligence (AI) technologies is expressly prohibited. HarperCollins also exercise their rights under Article 4(3) of the Digital Single Market Directive 2019/790 and expressly reserve this publication from the text and data mining exception.

Published by Collins
An imprint of HarperCollins*Publishers*
1 London Bridge Street
London SE1 9GF

HarperCollins*Publishers*
Macken House, 39/40 Mayor Street Upper,
Dublin 1, D01 C9W8, Ireland

© HarperCollins*Publishers* Limited 2025
ISBN 9780008727826
First published 2025
10 9 8 7 6 5 4 3 2 1

All rights reserved. No part of this publication may be reproduced, stored in a retrieval system, or transmitted, in any form or by any means, electronic, mechanical, photocopying, recording or otherwise, without the prior permission of Collins.

British Library Cataloguing in Publication Data.

A CIP record of this book is available from the British Library.

Publisher: Fiona McGlade
Author: Sasha Wigley
Contributors: Liz Dawson and Chris Parkinson
Project manager and editorial: Chantal Addy
Cover design: Sarah Duxbury
Inside concept design: Ian Wrigley
Text design and layout: SRM India
Artwork: Shutterstock and Collins
Production: Bethany Brohm
Printed in India by Multivista Global Pvt.Ltd.

MIX
Paper | Supporting responsible forestry
FSC™ C007454

Starter test

1. Think of **three** reasons why it is a good idea to play outside. Write them below.

    a) ....

    b) ....

    c) ....

    3 marks

2. Underline the words on each lily pad that contain the **digraph** on the frog.

    a) **ay** — stay enjoy away grew crayon

    b) **oe** — shell potatoes tiptoe drink goes

    c) **ir** — third twirl squirt phone birthday

    3 marks

3. Circle the words in each train that contain the sound **th**.

    a) shoes bath trap frog thunder

    b) snake tooth after ever three

c) thigh | train | catch | think | both

4. Tick the words that contain the **adjacent consonants** on the tile.

a) **gr**

giraffe ☐   grape ☐   going ☐   evergreen ☐

b) **st**

stamp ☐   sticker ☐   cold ☐   best ☐

c) **nd**

round ☐   them ☐   frog ☐   sandstorm ☐

5. Complete each word with the **digraph ph** or **wh**.

a) ……….ale

b) ……….otogra……….

c) tele……….one

d) ……….ich

e) ele……….ant

f) ……….isper

6. Read each sentence. Number the sentences **1–3** to show in what order they happen in *Little Red Riding Hood*.

The wolf pretends to be Grandma and tricks Little Red Riding Hood. ☐

Little Red Riding Hood sets off to Grandma's to take her some flowers. ☐

The woodcutter saves Little Red Riding Hood and Grandma. ☐

7. Read the paragraph. Answer the questions below.

> Dogs are loyal animals that have been kept as pets for thousands of years. They can be trained to do many jobs, like guiding people who cannot see or helping on farms. A dog's strong sense of smell makes it excellent at finding lost items or even people. Many dogs enjoy playing outside and need regular exercise to stay healthy.

a) Find the **adjective** in the first sentence that describes dogs.

....

b) Name **two** jobs that dogs can do.

....

....

c) What do dogs need to stay healthy?

....

....

4 marks

8. Draw a line to match each word ending to its missing letters. Then write the missing letters to complete the word.

Example: <u>br</u>ight

a) ....y

b) ....end

c) ....ash

fl

spl

bl

3 marks

9. Say what you see in each picture. Complete the word sum. The first one has been done for you.

> **Compound words** are made up of two shorter words.

a)  ...hand... + ...bag... = ...handbag...

b)  .... + ... = ...

c)  .... + ... = ...

d)  .... + ... = ...

e)  .... + ... = ...

4 marks

10. Join pairs of words with a line to make a **compound word**. Write the compound word.

a) **dough**   room   ....

b) **farm**   bridge   ....

c) **draw**   house   ....

d) **bath**   nut   ....

4 marks

11. Make **three compound words** of your own using these words.

a) tea + ... = ...

b) .... + bird = ...

c) sun + ... = ...

3 marks

Starter test 7

GPS 12. Write the **contracted form** of these words or phrases. The first one has been done for you.

a) it is = it's

b) have not = ...

c) cannot = ...

d) I am = ...

e) you are = ...

f) will not = ...

> An **apostrophe** can replace letters in order to shorten words. These **contractions** are less formal and easier to read.

5 marks

GPS 13. Read this paragraph and add **apostrophes** to show **contractions** in the correct places.

Id really like to go to the funfair on Sunday. Daisy told me that shed like to come too but she cant go until after lunch. If I went on my own it wouldnt be as much fun, so I think Ill wait for her.

5 marks

G 14. Write a sentence using each of these words correctly.

believe   question   appear

a) ....
....

b) ....
....

c) ....
....

3 marks

15. Add these **suffixes** to the words below to make new words. Write the new words in full.

-ful   -ment   -ness

a) enjoy................................ ....

b) help................................ ....

c) kind................................ ....

3 marks

16. Create words using the **prefixes** below, then write the new words.

arrange   agree   patient

a) dis + ... = ...

b) re + ... = ...

c) im + ... = ...

3 marks

17. Circle the correct **homophone** in each sentence.

a) The wild storm raged through the **knight** / **night**.

b) The teacher asked the boys to bring in **their** / **there** / **they're** homework.

c) We could **here** / **hear** the birds singing in the trees.

3 marks

18. Underline the **homophones** that have been spelled incorrectly in this paragraph.

The children were playing with there swords and shields. Ahmad wanted to be the brave night and Priya wanted to be the princess. They're mum could here them shouting and asked them to keep there voices down.

5 marks

19. Draw a line to match each sentence to the correct punctuation.

a) Why is the sky blue   !

b) The boys walked to the park   ?

c) How wonderful   .

3 marks

20. Circle the words that should always start with a **capital letter**. Explain why each word needs a capital. The first one has been done for you.

| saturday | england | pencil | january | dog |

a) Saturday starts with a capital letter because it is the name of a day of the week, which is a proper noun.

b) ....

c) ....

2 marks

21. Correct the punctuation in this paragraph. Mark in missing **capital letters**, **commas** and **full stops**.

on thursday tim and kira went for a walk with their dog billy it was cold and they had forgotten their hats so they did not stay out very long it was march after all!

14 marks

22. Circle the word in each pair that is written in the **past tense**.

a) fly / flew   b) run / ran

c) drive / drove   d) played / playing

e) swam / swim

5 marks

10

23. Write three sentences that use the **conjunction because** to join ideas.

a) ....

b) ....

c) ....

3 marks

24. Tick the sentences that use the **conjunction if** correctly to join ideas.

a) I will go outside if it stops raining. ☐

b) I will have a party if I am five. ☐

c) The flowers will bloom if the sun keeps shining. ☐

d) I will not go to school if I am poorly. ☐

e) We were late if the bus broke down. ☐

3 marks

25. Tick the **proper nouns**.

mouse ☐   dog ☐   Cornwall ☐

James ☐   Wednesday ☐   football ☐

3 marks

26. Fill each gap with an **adjective** to describe the noun.

a) The .... girl screamed and ran towards her friend.

1 mark

b) The sea was .... and ....

1 mark

c) The ...., ... spider ran across the floor.

1 mark

How am I doing?   Total marks: ☐ / 102

Starter test   11

Nouns and pronouns

Challenge 1

1. Write the **common noun** for each picture.

   a)  ....   b)  ....

   c)  ....   d)  ....

   e)  ....   f)  ....

   6 marks

2. Underline the **common noun** in each of these sentences.

   a) I sat beneath a tree.

   b) He walked along the river.

   c) Trevor threw the ball very high.

   3 marks

Challenge 2

1. Circle the **common nouns** and underline the **proper nouns** in these sentences.

   a) Sanjit went bowling with his friend, Andrei.

   b) In Scotland, there are lots of wild deer.

   c) On Saturday, Beth will go to visit her dad, who lives near the beach.

   9 marks

12

2. Underline the **pronoun** in each of these sentences. There may be more than one.

> A **pronoun** can replace a noun or noun phrase in a sentence.

a) He went for a walk.

b) You are a good friend.

c) They wrapped lots of presents.

d) I gave it to her.

e) We helped him.

8 marks

Challenge 3

1. Read the **nouns** in the box below. Write each **noun** in the list under the correct heading.

> November   glass   we   Marcus
> them   book   Scotland   she

Common nouns

....

....

....

Proper nouns

....

....

....

Pronouns

....

....

....

8 marks

How am I doing?   Total marks: / 34

Verbs

Challenge 1

1 There are **five verbs** in the wordsearch below. Use the pictures to help you find them. Words can go forwards, backwards, up or down.

a	o	r	u	m	s	t	a
i	h	s	r	u	n	w	s
p	h	p	f	h	l	d	w
r	c	w	o	d	e	i	i
s	t	o	h	i	k	n	m
e	a	t	w	i	n	t	n
b	w	c	z	l	t	e	v
a	n	s	p	i	k	s	y

1. ....
2. ....
3. ....
4. ....
5. ....

5 marks

Challenge 2

1 Underline the **verb** in each sentence.

a) Tyler jogged home.

b) Rosina played outside with her friends.

c) The dogs barked at the squirrels.

d) I am happy.

e) Tomorrow, James will go to the cinema.

5 marks

14

2 Write a **verb** in each gap to complete the sentences.

a) After school, Ali .... TV.

b) Jason .... a book to his Dad.

c) Jan .... an apple.

3 marks

Challenge 3

1 Read the paragraph below. Underline the **twelve verbs**, then write them on the lines.

> The ancient Egyptians lived along the River Nile in Egypt. They grew crops like wheat and barley and ate bread, vegetables and fish. Men and women sometimes wore jewellery to show their status. For fun, they liked board games, danced and made music with harps and flutes. Children played with toys like dolls and balls. The Egyptians built temples, created beautiful art, and honoured their gods with ceremonies and festivals.

....

....

....

....

....

....

12 marks

How am I doing? Total marks: /25

Grammar 15

Present perfect form of verbs

Challenge 1

1 Circle the **two** correct words to complete each sentence.

a) Angus **has** / **have**   **swinged** / **swung** the bat.

b) I **has** / **have**   **drink** / **drunk** all the orange juice.

c) The dog **has** / **have**   **caught** / **catched** the ball.

d) Ricardo **has** / **have**   **watch** / **watched** the football game on TV.

e) Monika **has** / **have**   **washed** / **wash** the dishes in the cottage.

f) The boys **has** / **have**   **dipped** / **dip** their biscuits in their tea.

g) The referee **has** / **have**   **blowed** / **blown** her whistle too loudly.

h) My brother and I **has** / **have**   **collect** / **collected** conkers since we were four.

8 marks

Challenge 2

1 Complete the sentences using **has** or **have** so that they make sense in the **present perfect tense**.

a) The birds .... sung all day.

b) She .... watched television all evening.

c) We .... supported our team for five years.

d) The nurse .... worked there since she was twenty years old.

e) The wind .... blown strongly all day.

f) The dogs .... howled all night.

g) We .... watched that programme since it started.

h) They .... always wanted to visit this museum.

8 marks

2 Tick to show whether the sentences are in the **past tense** or the **present perfect tense**.

	Past	Present perfect
a) Dad braked to stop the car.	☐	☐
b) Dad has braked to stop the car.	☐	☐
c) I have been at this school for two years.	☐	☐
d) He was at the school two years ago.	☐	☐

4 marks

Challenge 3

1 Complete these sentences.

a) I have wished for ....

b) The child has sung ....

c) We have walked ....

d) They have wanted a puppy ....

4 marks

2 Fill in the gaps with the **present perfect tense** using the **verb** in brackets.

a) I .... (**decorate**) the house for Mum's birthday.

b) You .... (**read**) three books about stars.

c) She .... (**play**) the piano since she was six.

d) They .... (**score**) three goals since half time.

e) The sun .... (**shine**) all day.

5 marks

How am I doing?   Total marks: ☐ / 29

Grammar 17

Adverbs

Challenge 1

1. Underline the **verb**. Circle the **adverb** in each sentence.

   > An **adverb** can describe **how** the **verb** takes place.

   a) Saskia bravely fought the dragon.

   b) Chadi used the scissors carefully.

   4 marks

2. Complete each sentence using one of the **adverbs** from the box below.

   happily   slowly   fantastically

   a) The tortoise plodded .... back home.

   b) You performed .... in the school play.

   c) The dog wagged its tail ....

   3 marks

Challenge 2

1. Circle the **adverb** in each sentence below that describes the verb 'to sing'.

   > An **adverb** can also describe **when or how often** the **verb** takes place.

   a) Finally, he sang his wonderful song.

   b) I usually sing in assembly.

   c) Today, Lucy wants to sing with the choir.

   d) Rupert never sings.

   e) We sang six songs yesterday.

   5 marks

18

2 Draw a line to match the beginning of the sentence to the correct **adverb**.

> An **adverb** can describe **where** the **verb** takes place.

When it's sunny, Sue prefers to eat — anywhere.

Place your empty plate — here.

I can sleep — outside.

3 marks

Challenge 3

1 Use each **adverb** in a sentence. Write your sentence on the lines.

a) always ....

....

b) later ....

....

c) beautifully ....

....

d) upstairs ....

....

4 marks

How am I doing?   Total marks: / 19

Conjunctions

Challenge 1

1. Tick the sentences that use the correct **conjunction**. The conjunction is in bold.

   > A **conjunction** can be used to join two clauses together.

   a) It was raining **so** I put up my umbrella.

   b) Chaz visited the sweet shop **nor** he went to the toy shop.

   c) It was a very cold day **yet** the sun was shining.

   d) Mrs Chen liked running **but** she preferred tennis.

   3 marks

2. Rewrite the sentences using one of the **conjunctions** in the box below.

   but   and   or

   a) I could use the front door. I could use the kitchen door.

   ....

   b) His dog loves puddles. He hates getting wet.

   ....

   c) Max is five years old. His sister is ten.

   ....

   3 marks

Challenge 2

1. Fill each gap with the correct **conjunction**.

   because   if   so

   a) Marnie finished her homework .... she got a gold star.

b) You might be sick .... you eat too many sweets.

c) My mum was angry .... we broke her vase.

3 marks

2. These sentences all use **conjunctions**. Draw a line to match the start and end of each sentence.

a) I am lucky   yet they are so far away.

b) I can see the full moon   because I got a telescope for my birthday.

c) The stars look so close   when I use my telescope.

3 marks

Challenge 3

1. Use the **conjunctions** from the box to complete the paragraph.

because   if   so   although   while

Lions are known as the kings of the jungle .... they are powerful predators with no natural enemies. They are often portrayed as solitary hunters .... lions are actually social animals that live in prides. .... a lion pride works together, they can take down large prey like buffalo or giraffes, providing enough food for everyone. The lionesses are usually responsible for hunting .... the males often defend the pride. Lions take turns eating .... even the cubs have a chance to feed.

5 marks

How am I doing?   Total marks: ☐ /17

Grammar   21

Conjunctions to show time (when)

Challenge 1

1. Choose from the **time conjunctions** below to complete the sentences.

   Time conjunctions are used to connect two actions or events and show the time relationship between them.

   | before | after | as soon as | when | then |

   a) I climbed into bed .... brushing my teeth.

   b) The train pulled up at the station, ... let the passengers off.

   c) I scratch my dog's tummy .... she rolls on her back.

   d) Zac washed his hands .... eating his sandwich.

   e) Dad drank his cup of tea .... it had cooled down.

   5 marks

Challenge 2

1. Circle the **time conjunctions** in the paragraph below.

   Sam packed his backpack with snacks, a water bottle and his favourite binoculars before heading to the zoo. Then he hopped into the car with his parents, excitedly chatting about the animals he wanted to see. Next, they arrived at the zoo's entrance where he eagerly handed over the tickets. They decided to visit the lions after visiting the ape enclosure. Sam stopped during their walk to watch the playful monkeys. Soon it was time for lunch and they strolled to the picnic area.

   6 marks

2 Put these instructions for making a cup of tea in order from 1–6. Write the number in the box.

> **Time conjunctions** are helpful when writing instructions.

a) ☐ Before pouring in the milk, remove the tea bag.

b) ☐ First, boil the kettle by flicking the switch.

c) ☐ Then put a tea bag in a mug.

d) ☐ Next, add a splash of milk.

e) ☐ The tea will soon be ready to drink but you may want to leave it to cool.

f) ☐ After the kettle has boiled, fill the mug with hot water.

6 marks

Challenge 3

1 Now write your own set of instructions for making a jam sandwich. Use the **time conjunctions** below. Start a new line for each instruction. Remember to number each instruction.

| after | first | before | next | then |

....

....

....

....

....

5 marks

How am I doing? 😐 🙂 😃

Total marks: ☐ /22

Grammar 23

Prepositions

Challenge 1

1 Use each picture to help you identify the **preposition**.

a)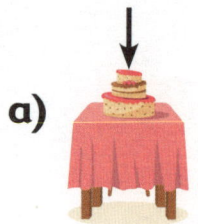

....

b)

....

c)

....

d)

....

4 marks

2 Underline the **preposition** in each sentence below.

a) The apple was put on the table.

b) The dog hid in its basket.

c) The boy climbed over the fence.

d) The presents were put under the Christmas tree.

4 marks

Challenge 2

1 Circle the **prepositions** in the sentences below.

a) The train rushed through the tunnel.

b) The sun set above the mountains.

c) The children had a picnic by the river.

d) Beneath the tree was a pile of leaves.

4 marks

2 Tick each **preposition**.

under ☐	over ☐	went ☐
beneath ☐	above ☐	ran ☐
green ☐	sat ☐	through ☐

5 marks

Challenge 3

1 Find the **prepositions** in the wordsearch below. Words can go forwards, backwards, up or down.

below   within   through   in
over   above   under   beneath

t	h	r	o	u	g	h
b	b	a	w	t	h	o
e	e	i	i	n	s	v
n	l	a	b	o	v	e
e	o	t	h	r	o	r
a	s	u	n	d	e	r
t	w	i	t	h	i	n
h	b	e	l	o	w	n

8 marks

2 Underline all the **prepositions** in the paragraph below.

Yesterday, Ben went on a train. The journey was spectacular. The train went through lots of tunnels and even went over a bridge. Ben enjoyed looking out of the window at all of the beautiful scenery. He watched the sun rise high in the sky, above a castle, and he watched the waves of the sea below the train track.

7 marks

How am I doing?   Total marks: ☐ /32

Grammar 25

Determiners

Challenge 1

1. Write the correct **determiner** a or an for each picture. The first one has been done for you.

   a)

   a cup

   b) ....

   c)

   ....

   d) ....

   e)

   ....

   f)

   ....

2. Write the correct **determiner** a or an for each noun below.

   a) .... banana   b) .... shoe   c) .... orange

Challenge 2

1. Circle the correct **determiner** for the noun phrases below.

   a) a / an yellow bus

   b) a / an open window

   c) an / a giant octopus

   d) an / a immense hippopotamus

   e) a / an fantastic achievement

26

2 Fill in the correct **determiner** using **a** or **an** to complete each sentence.

a) Yesterday, I went to ………… beach.

b) For my lunch, I ate ………… apple after my sandwich.

c) For my birthday, I got ………… amazing present.

d) ………… octopus has eight legs.

e) She went on ………… train.

5 marks

Challenge 3

1 Complete the sentences below by adding a **noun** or an **adjective**.

a) At the cinema I saw an ……………………………… film.

b) On the beach I found a ……………………………… .

c) There was an ……………………………… at the zoo.

3 marks

2 Complete the paragraph below by writing **a** or **an** in each gap.

During my visit to the zoo, I saw lots of animals. My favourite was ………… Arctic polar bear. It was huge and had ………… massive jaw. It spent most of its time sleeping in ………… cave but occasionally it swam around in ………… pool. For its dinner it was fed ………… enormous fish, which it gobbled up in one go. I also loved seeing the elephants. One was ………… baby elephant. It had ………… extraordinary trunk. It looked far too big for its body!

7 marks

How am I doing?   Total marks: / 28

Grammar   27

Capital letters and full stops

Challenge 1

1 Read the words below. Write the words that should start with a **capital letter** on the numbered lines.

april	sunday
pudding	portugal
feet	computer
mr wood	ethan

1. ....
2. ....
3. ....
4. ....
5. ....

5 marks

2 Circle the words in the paragraph below that should start with a **capital letter**.

> Last tuesday, i moved to a new house on west road. I share a room with my little brother james. You can see wembley stadium from the window. In june, we're going to see the england team play wales.

10 marks

Challenge 2

1 Rewrite each sentence, adding **capital letters** in the correct place.

a) When i was twelve, i visited london.

....

b) Bill and jenny went on holiday to spain in september.

....

6 marks

28

Challenge 3

1. Read the postcard below. Add the missing **capital letters** and **full stops**.

dear mrs porter,

i am having a lovely weekend in france i arrived on thursday and am not back until august yesterday we went shopping mum says it's going to rain tomorrow

see you soon

mrs porter

milford school

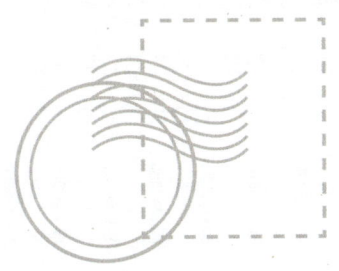

20 marks

2. Look at each picture. Write a sentence to describe each animal using **capital letters** and **full stops** in the correct places.

a)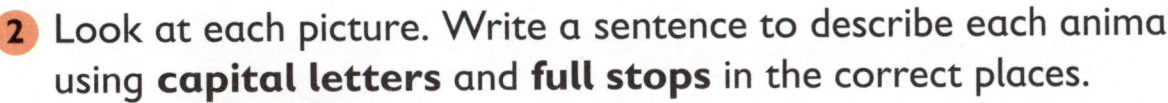

b)

c)

3 marks

How am I doing? 😐 🙂 😃   Total marks: ☐ /44

Punctuation 29

Commas for lists

Challenge 1

1. Write the items from this shopping list in one sentence, using **commas** to separate the items in the list.

   Shopping list:

   1 pack of bacon

   6 eggs

   4 sausages

   2 tins of beans

   1 loaf of bread

   At the shop, we need to buy:

   ....

   ....

   ....

   ....

   3 marks

Challenge 2

1. Punctuate these sentences with **commas** to separate the adjectives.

   a) The girl had long curly golden hair.

   b) It was a cold grey drizzly morning.

   c) The fire was blue orange and red.

   d) The wood was damp dark and mysterious.

   e) His eyes were blue piercing and trustworthy.

   f) The petals were colourful soft and scented.

   6 marks

30

2 Punctuate these sentences with **commas** in the lists.

a) From the market, Zayn bought three bananas a bunch of grapes and some ham.

b) The recipe needed two eggs plain flour and sugar.

c) Ben tidied up his toy cars his train track his art set and his dominoes.

d) In Sam's money box, he had some pound coins twenty pence pieces five pence pieces and pennies.

e) In the baby's cot there was a rattle a dummy and a soft toy.

f) Last night I ate a pie some chips and a pudding.

6 marks

Challenge 3

1 Add the missing **commas** to the paragraph below.

Bobby had to go to the shop with his mum. He wouldn't have minded but the shop was cold boring and a long way away. The shopping list was not very long, so on the way they decided to stop at the park. He went on the swings the slide and the roundabout. The walk to the shop was quite interesting, especially as he saw three of his friends a really cute dog and a rabbit running across the field. When they finally got to the shop, they bought the items quickly. They got oranges apples bananas and kiwi fruits. They also bought some carrots green beans and tomatoes. On the way home, he was hungry and decided to try one of the apples. It was sweet juicy and crispy. It tasted delicious!

7 marks

How am I doing?

Total marks: /22

Punctuation 31

Apostrophes for contractions

Challenge 1

1. Draw a line to match each **contraction** to the complete words.

wasn't		will not
can't		I will
won't		would not
I'll		was not
wouldn't		cannot

   5 marks

2. Write the **contractions** of these word pairs.

   a) it is .... b) he is ....

   c) they are .... d) we have ....

   e) should not .... f) is not ....

   6 marks

Challenge 2

1. Find the **contractions** of these words in the wordsearch. The words can run up or down.

w	'	a	t	h	n	t	s
s	w	w	a	s	n	'	t
s	a	e	'	e	h	n	'
h	e	'	l	l	t	d	n
d	f	v	h	'	s	l	a
a	w	e	t	n	e	u	c
r	'	o	'	n	g	o	'
l	'	t	r	v	m	c	s
w	o	u	l	d	n	'	t

   was not
   would not
   could not
   cannot
   he will
   we have

   6 marks

32

Challenge 3

1 Complete the paragraph below with the most suitable **contractions** from the box.

| didn't | shouldn't | I've | don't | it's | I'll |

I love going to the cinema! .... been excited about seeing this film for weeks! I hope I .... forget to bring my ticket. .... get some popcorn and a drink before it starts. You .... talk during the film because .... important to let everyone enjoy it. Wow, I .... realise the film was so long!

6 marks

2 Write **four** of your own sentences using **contractions** from the box in question 1.

a) ....

b) ....

c) ....

d) ....

4 marks

How am I doing?   Total marks: ___ /27

Punctuation 33

Possessive apostrophes

Challenge 1

1. Add **'s** to these **singular** nouns to show possession.

   Example: The bone belonging to the dog is the **dog's** bone.

   a) boy   b) cat   c) girl   d) sheep   e) rabbit

   ....

   5 marks

2. Choose a word from question 1 to complete each sentence.

   a) The .... dress was torn.

   b) The .... field was extremely muddy.

   c) The .... hat got blown away in the wind.

   d) The .... tail became trapped in the door.

   e) The .... burrow was invaded by ants.

   5 marks

Challenge 2

1. Underline the correct use of an **apostrophe** to show **plural** possession.

   Example: The tails belonging to the dogs are the <u>dogs'</u> tails.

   a) The **pupils'** / **pupil's** school was closed because of the snow.

   b) The **tree's** / **trees'** branches waved in the wind.

   c) The **boy's** / **boys'** trainers were filthy.

   3 marks

2. Read each sentence. Does the underlined noun show **singular** or **plural** possession? The first one has been done for you.

   a) The <u>girl's</u> hair was tied up in a ponytail.   ....*singular*........

b) The <u>horses'</u> stables were freezing cold. ....

c) The woman brushed the <u>dogs'</u> fur. ....

d) The <u>book's</u> pages were torn. ....

3 marks

Challenge 3

1. Use **apostrophes** to show possession for the nouns below.

   a) **1 shop** — The shop.......... window was broken.

   b) **4 boys** — The boy.......... trousers were muddy from playing football.

   c) **1 mum** — I went in my mum.......... new car.

   3 marks

2. Choose from the nouns below to fill the gaps in the paragraph. Use **apostrophes** to show either **singular** or **plural** possession.

   boy   dog   brother   mum   tree

   I went to the .... house after school today. I got to go in his .... new car. It was funny because I accidentally stood in the .... water bowl and my foot was soaking wet. I also played with his .... toys. Afterwards, we went in the garden. All of the .... leaves had fallen off and we stamped our feet through them on the ground.

   5 marks

How am I doing?   Total marks: /24

Punctuation 35

Using inverted commas for direct speech

Challenge 1

1. Add in the **inverted commas** to show what is being said. The first one has been done for you.

   a) "I'm so hungry!" b) That's fantastic news.

   c) I had a brilliant weekend. d) Sit down everyone!

   3 marks

2. Add in the missing **inverted commas** to show the direct speech.

   a) Stop that!" shouted Jacob.

   b) I was so frightened," explained Maya to her best friend.

   c) Why didn't you tell me before?" asked Mum.

   d) If only you knew the full story," Rory whispered.

   e) I've lost my pencil," Bessie told the teacher.

   5 marks

3. Add in the missing **inverted commas** to show the direct speech.

   a) "Remember not to go near the bonfire, Dad warned.

   b) "It's my birthday soon, Sebastian said excitedly.

   c) "Don't be too late back, Grandpa called.

   d) "Friday is my favourite day of the week, Amin told Owen.

   e) "I don't like peas! shouted Carlos.

   5 marks

Challenge 2

1. Tick the correctly punctuated sentences.

   a) Blake said, "I love going fishing."

   b) "Finn shrieked, this is great!"

   c) I don't want to fish, explained Layla. "I don't like fishing."

36

d) "Please may I have a turn"? asked Abdullah.

e) "Please be careful," warned Mum.
"It's very dangerous."

2 Add in the **inverted commas** to show the direct speech.

a) Today is going to be so much fun, yelled Panjit.

b) Lily whispered, Has it gone yet?

c) I'm not sure about this at all! moaned Ed.

d) I love swimming, explained Belinda. I'm quite good at it too!

e) I'm tired, said Hamish. At least we can rest when we get home.

Challenge 3

1 Insert the missing punctuation in this paragraph. There are **four inverted commas**, **one full stop** and **one question mark** missing.

.... Is it nearly time to go .... " asked Horace.

"I hope so, ... replied Alfie .... I'm so excited."

"I think it will be even better than we think!......... shrieked Horace.

2 Insert all the missing punctuation in this paragraph.

When I get home I'm going to have a big drink of water said Megan. I'm very thirsty!

"It's been a great day but I'm exhausted now Bethan replied

"Shall we go again tomorrow" Megan asked.

Definitely! shouted Bethan.

How am I doing?   Total marks:

Punctuation   37

Progress test 1

1. Circle the **verb** in each sentence below.

    a) The tall tree leaned to the right.

    b) The girl shouted to her friend.

    c) Patrick rode his bike to school.

    d) I went to the cinema.

    e) The sun slipped behind the mountains.

    5 marks

2. Underline the **preposition** in each sentence below.

    a) There was a bowl of fruit on the table.

    b) A wolf howled beneath the full moon.

    c) Above the crowds of people, the planes flew noisily.

    d) The actor waited patiently behind the curtain.

    4 marks

3. Contract these words using an **apostrophe**.

    a) you are ....

    b) I am ....

    c) they are ....

    d) are not ....

    e) she will ....

    5 marks

4. Fill in the gaps with the **determiner a** or **an**.

> Dinosaur eggs often had .... oval shape and .... unusual texture on their shell. They could be as small as .... orange or as big as .... watermelon! Can you imagine finding .... amazing egg like that? Today, you might see one in .... museum.

6 marks

5. Add the missing **commas** to each sentence below.

a) I need a loaf of bread a tomato and some cheese.

b) My cousin likes football tennis netball and swimming.

c) There was a roundabout a burger stall a coconut shy and a ghost train at the funfair.

d) Mum and Dad bought pizza doughnuts cakes sweets and jelly for the party.

8 marks

6. Add a **conjunction** from the box to each of the sentences so that they make sense.

> **so**   **because**   **if**   **when**

a) Charlie felt really tired .... he went to bed late last night.

b) I wanted an ice cream .... I asked my mum politely.

c) .... I saw a spider, it made me jump.

d) "I will be proud .... you try your best," said Mrs Wigley.

4 marks

Progress test 1

7. Add the **inverted commas** to these sentences to show speech.

a) I want my dinner, cried Billy.

b) The teacher asked, Where is your homework?

c) Take your medicine every morning, said the kind doctor.

d) Did you see the train? asked Stanley, It was fantastic.

4 marks

8. Add an **apostrophe** in the correct place in each sentence to show **singular** possession.

a) The boys tooth fell out.

b) The hamster bit the girls finger.

c) Mums glasses smashed into pieces on the floor.

d) The cheeky cat drank Marys tea.

4 marks

9. Circle the correct word so that each sentence makes sense in the **present perfect** tense.

a) The snowflakes **have** / **has** fallen and covered the lawn.

b) John **have** / **has** enjoyed painting since he was young.

c) All the children **have** / **has** eaten their fruit.

d) One robin **have** / **has** visited the bird feeder.

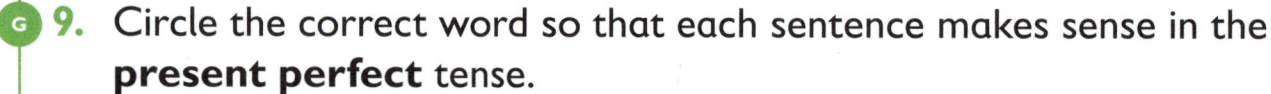

4 marks

10. Circle all the **time conjunctions** below.

then	because	if	before
soon	next	so	
when	and	after	

6 marks

11. Add an **apostrophe** in the correct place in each sentence to show **plural** possession.

a) 50 cows — The cows milk was taken to the shop to be sold.

b) 3 horses — The horses stables were cleaned out.

c) 2 chickens — Every day, I collect the chickens eggs.

3 marks

12. Write each word from the box into the correct column.

house   January   star   apple   Australia   walking stick   Martha   The Lion King

Common nouns	Proper nouns

8 marks

13. a) Underline all the **pronouns** in the sentences below.

Emily said she would help her brother with his homework because he was struggling.

b) Replace the underlined words with suitable **pronouns**.

Liam and Sarah took <u>Liam and Sarah's</u> dog for a walk, and then <u>Liam and Sarah</u> played with <u>the dog</u> in the garden.

7 marks

How am I doing?   Total marks: ___ / 68

Progress test 1   41

Prefixes 1

Challenge 1

1. Draw a line to match each **prefix** to the correct root word.

   un — appropriate
   in — lead
   dis — clear
   mis — advantage

   4 marks

2. The words below begin with the **prefixes im-, il- or ir-**. Split each word into its prefix and root word.

   a) imperfect = ... + ...

   b) illogical = ... + ...

   c) irresistible = ... + ...

   d) irregular = ... + ...

   e) impossible = ... + ...

   f) illegal = ... + ...

   6 marks

3. Draw a line to match the correct meaning to each **prefix**.

   re — by itself
   auto — again
   anti — against

   3 marks

42

Challenge 2

1. The underlined words in the sentences all start with a **prefix**. Write the meaning of each word on the line.

   a) The work was left <u>unfinished</u> by the builder.

   ....

   b) The child <u>misread</u> the sign on the wall.

   ....

   c) Cheeky dogs <u>disobey</u> their owners' commands.

   ....

   d) The accident happened at a very <u>inconvenient</u> time.

   ....

   4 marks

Challenge 3

1. Use your dictionary to find the meaning of the words in the clouds. Then write each word in a sentence.

   immortal   illiterate   irresponsible

   a) ....

   ....

   b) ....

   ....

   c) ....

   ....

   3 marks

How am I doing?   Total marks: ☐ /20

Spelling   43

Prefixes 2

Challenge 1

1. Underline the **prefix** in each of the words in the boxes. Then match each word to its meaning.

   anticlockwise — to write something again

   automatic — moving in the opposite direction to the way the hands on a clock move

   rewrite — working by itself with little or no direct human control

   3 marks

Challenge 2

1. Join a **prefix** with a **root word** to create a new word. Write the new words on the lines below.

Prefix	Root word
mis	gravity
un	take
ir	comfortable
anti	rational
auto	graph

   a) .... b) ....

   c) .... d) ....

   e) ....

   5 marks

44

Challenge 3

1 The following words each contain a **prefix**. Complete each of the sentences using one of the words below.

| automatic | disallowed | antibiotics |
| reintroduced | misunderstood | irreversible |

a) Tottenham's goal was .... because it was offside.

b) At a party, I was .... to someone I had met before.

c) I was given .... to fight off my illness.

d) We bought an .... car.

e) Breaking a glass is .... because you can't put it back together again.

f) Naomi .... the instructions and went to the wrong classroom.

6 marks

2 Choose a **prefix** from the box to complete the paragraph.

| in | im | un | dis | re |

The school trip to the zoo was almost ruined by the ....expected rain. It was ....possible to see the animals through the fogged-up windows of the bus. Some of the children felt it was ....appointing, especially since the trip had been planned for months. We had to leave early which meant the children's work was ....complete. Hopefully, the teacher will be able to ....schedule the trip.

5 marks

How am I doing?   Total marks: ___/19

Spelling 45

Suffixes 1

Challenge 1

1. Copy each adjective and add the **suffix -ly** to make an adverb.

   a) proud   b) sudden   c) strange   d) peaceful

   ....

   4 marks

2. Write a sentence using each of the **adverbs** you have written in question 1. The first one has been done for you.

   a) The athlete collected their award **proudly**.

   b) ....

   c) ....

   d) ....

   3 marks

Challenge 2

1. Complete the table below. Notice how the ending of the adjective affects the spelling of its adverb.

Adjective	Adverb
	happily
angry	
	gently
simple	
	basically
dramatic	

6 marks

46

Challenge 3

1. Underline the **suffix** in each of these adjectives.

   a) vari<u>ous</u>

   b) mountain<u>ous</u>

   c) horrend<u>ous</u>

   d) danger<u>ous</u>

   e) poison<u>ous</u>

   f) courage<u>ous</u>

2. Draw a line to match each word to its correct definition.

fabulous	extremely unpleasant
jealous	extraordinary or wonderful
obvious	feeling resentment for what other people have
hideous	easy to see, understand or recognise

3. Circle the correct spelling of the words ending in the **suffix** -ous.

   a) serious / seriuos

   b) enormous / enormus

   c) gloryous / glorious

   d) joyous / joious

   e) ridiculus / ridiculous

How am I doing?   Total marks: ☐ / 28

Suffixes 2

Challenge 1

1 Use the **suffix -ture** or **-sure** to complete each word. Say the word and listen to how the suffix sounds.

a)  pic......................

b)  mea......................

2 marks

2 Read the words with the **suffixes -ture** or **-sure**. Circle the odd one out in each line.

a) adventure   capture   pressure

b) treasure   mixture   pleasure

c) nature   future   closure

3 marks

Challenge 2

1 Complete each word below with the **suffix -ture** or **-sure**.

a) crea......................   b) frac......................

c) sculp......................   d) furni......................

e) enclo......................   f) lei......................

6 marks

48

2 Use the words from the box below to complete the sentences.

| treasure | nature | creature | pleasure |

a) The fearsome .... was guarding the .... in the cave.

b) My favourite .... in life is to walk among ....

4 marks

Challenge 3

1 Read the words on the pencils. Write a sentence including each word.

a) **dangerously** ▶ ....

....

b) **curiously** ▶ ....

....

c) **outrageously** ▶ ....

....

d) **ferociously** ▶ ....

....

4 marks

How am I doing?   Total marks: ☐ / 19

Root words

Challenge 1

1. Draw a line from each word to its **root word**.

   a) searching — agree
   b) dropped — search
   c) disagree — play
   d) replay — drop

   4 marks

2. Add **one** of these **suffixes** to each **root word** to make a new word. The first one has been done for you.

   | -ing | -er | -est | -ed | -ly |

   a) fall + ..ing.. = ..falling..
   b) jump + ... = ...
   c) high + ... = ...
   d) low + ... = ...
   e) brilliant + ... = ...

   4 marks

Challenge 2

1. Use the **root words** and the **prefixes** in the table to create new words. The first one has been done for you.

Root word	Prefix	New word
a) market	super	supermarket
b) behave	mis	
c) way	sub	
d) correct	in	

   3 marks

2 Use the **root words** and the **suffixes** in the table to create new words. The first one has been done for you.

Root word	Suffix	New word
a) bright	en	brighten
b) danger	ous	
c) amaze	ment	
d) care	ful	

3 marks

Challenge 3

1 Read the list of **root words** in the boxes. Find the word from the same word family in the wordsearch and write it below. The first one has been done for you.

- fast
- confuse
- act
- soft
- direct
- create
- pilot

c	r	e	a	t	i	o	n	l	z
o	q	i	s	o	f	t	l	y	r
n	d	m	n	i	f	v	o	n	e
f	o	u	r	t	z	q	j	e	d
u	f	a	s	t	e	s	t	h	i
s	l	l	h	a	g	r	d	o	r
i	b	c	p	e	f	t	a	n	e
o	e	t	w	i	y	z	k	c	c
n	a	u	t	o	p	i	l	o	t

fastest

6 marks

How am I doing?   　　Total marks: /20

Exception words

Challenge 1

1. Add the **suffix -ing** or **-ed** to these **root words**. You will need to double the final consonant in the root word. The first one has been done for you.

Root word	+	Suffix	New word
a) flap	+	ed	flapped
b) fit	+	ing	
c) prefer	+	ed	
d) begin	+	ing	

3 marks

2. Circle the correct spelling in each pair of words.

   a) slip ⟶ slipping / sliping

   b) jump ⟶ jumped / jumpped

   c) sit ⟶ sitting / siting

3 marks

Challenge 2

1. Complete the table below. Remember to double the consonant after a vowel in the **root word** before adding the **suffix**.

Root word	Suffix	New word
a)	ing	clapping
travel	er	b)
c)	d)	spotted
stop	ed	e)
begin	er	f)

6 marks

52

Challenge 3

1. Write some words of your own that have the **suffix -ing** or **-ed**. Some may have double consonants.

   a) ....

   b) ....

   c) ....

   3 marks

2. Write a sentence using each of these words.

   forgetting   controlled   grinned

   a) ....
   ....

   b) ....
   ....

   c) ....
   ....

   3 marks

How am I doing?   Total marks: ☐ / 18

Etymology – the origin of words

> Many English words that we use today originate from other languages and therefore use some of their spellings and sounds.
> For example, words that use the digraph **ch** for the **k** sound come from Greek.

Challenge 1

1. Draw a line to match each word to its meaning.

   echo — a person or place you can buy medicine from

   character — a repeating sound

   chemist — a person in a book, film or play

   Say the words aloud. Can you hear the **k** sound in these words?

   3 marks

Challenge 2

1. Tick the words that use **ch** to make the **sh** sound.

   > Words that use the digraph **ch** for the **sh** sound come from French.
   > For example: **chef**.

chocolate ☐	children ☐
machine ☐	moustache ☐
cheese ☐	chute ☐
brochure ☐	French ☐
change ☐	

   CHOCOLATE BONBONS

   4 marks

54

2. **a)** Say the words **scenery**, **scent**, **scissors**. What do you notice about the **c** in these words?

....

....

....

> Words that use the digraph **sc** for the **s** sound come from the ancient language of Latin. For example: **scene**.

1 mark

b) Draw lines to match the words to their origins.

science		French (**sh** sound)
chorus		Latin (**s** sound)
parachute		Greek (**k** sound)

3 marks

Challenge 3

1. Put a tick in the correct column to show which words match the sounds **g** and **k**.

> Some English words end in **-gue** and **-que**. Many of them come from **French**.

	g	k
a) league		
b) cheque		
c) antique		
d) vague		

4 marks

How am I doing?

Total marks: ___ / 15

Spelling 55

Morphology – the formation of words

Challenge 1

1 Use your knowledge of **root words** to match each word with its meaning.

- misplace
- illegal
- disappear
- irregular

- not legal
- to lose something
- not regular
- vanish from view

4 marks

2 Add a **root word** from the box below to each **prefix** to create a new word. Then draw a line from each new word to its correct meaning.

agree   understand   changed

a) dis_____

b) un_____

c) mis_____

- not understand
- not agree
- not changed

6 marks

Challenge 2

1 Read the sentences and use your knowledge of **prefixes** and **root words** to help you to find the meaning of each underlined word. Tick the box that shows the correct meaning.

a) The child's homework was <u>incomplete</u>.

finished ☐   not finished ☐

b) The cat was <u>uncertain</u> about the new puppy.

not sure ☐   excited ☐

c) He was in a lot of <u>discomfort</u> after his fall.

worry ☐   pain ☐

2 Match each **prefix** to a suitable **root word** so that the new word has the opposite meaning.

| capable | town | able | breathe |

dis-   un-   mis-   in-

| catch | friendly | eat | match |

Challenge 3

1 Write a sentence using each word below to show that you know what it means.

impatient   misspell   disobey

a) ....

....

b) ....

....

c) ....

....

How am I doing?   Total marks: ☐ / 20

Homophones

> **Homophones** are words that sound the same but have a different spelling and meaning.

Challenge 1

1 Write a **homophone** for each word.

a) see ....

b) mail ....

c) son ....

d) bee ....

e) one ....

f) groan ....

g) blue ....

h) two ....

8 marks

Challenge 2

1 Draw a line to match each word with its meaning.

berry	to shout out
bury	an award for bravery or winning a race
ball	a small, juicy fruit
bawl	to interfere with something
medal	to put in the ground and cover with earth
meddle	a sphere

6 marks

Challenge 3

1. Add the words from the boxes to complete each sentence correctly.

   a) **heal / heel**   The blister on my .... took some time to ....

   b) **missed / mist**   We .... our turning because the road sign was hidden by the ....

   c) **break / brake**   Mum uses the .... when she is driving to make sure she does not .... the speed limit.

   d) **not / knot**   I could .... undo the .... in my shoelace.

   e) **scene / seen**   When we had .... the last .... of the play, everyone clapped.

   5 marks

2. Write sentences of your own using these **homophones**.

   a) **peace** ▶ ....

   ....

   b) **piece** ▶ ....

   ....

   c) **hear** ▶ ....

   ....

   d) **here** ▶ ....

   ....

   4 marks

How am I doing?   Total marks: ___ /23

Common misspellings

Challenge 1

1 Circle the correct spelling in each pair of words.

a) because / becoz	b) froot / fruit

c) February / Febuary	d) surprise / sprise

e) bizzy / busy	f) imajin / imagine

g) cort / caught	h) through / throo

8 marks

2 Tick the words that are spelled correctly.

happened ☐	groop ☐	bought ☐

swiming ☐	come ☐	nite ☐

once ☐	where ☐	bicycle ☐

6 marks

Challenge 2

1 Place each word below into the correct column in the table. Then correct the misspelled words.

| decided | frightend | started | getting |
| anuther | answer | thort | famus |

Correct spelling	Incorrect spelling	Corrected spelling

4 marks

60

Challenge 3

1. Circle the correct spelling so that the passage makes sense.

   Sophie couldn't **beleve** / **believe** it was **Monday** / **Munday** again. "I **allways** / **always** wish the weekend was longer," she said / **sed** with a sigh. "I **carn't** / **can't** wait to do **something** / **sumthing** fun."

   6 marks

2. Read the words in the box below. Write a sentence including each one.

   | truly | richer | eight | tongue | babies |

   a) ....

   b) ....

   c) ....

   d) ....

   e) ....

   5 marks

How am I doing?   Total marks: ☐ /29

Vowels and consonants

Challenge 1

1. Circle all the **vowels** in the alphabet.

    abcdefghijklmnopqrstuvwxyz

2. Circle all the **consonants** in the alphabet.

    abcdefghijklmnopqrstuvwxyz

5 marks

5 marks

Challenge 2

1. Join the **vowels** in alphabetical order. Start and end at the red **a** and move clockwise.

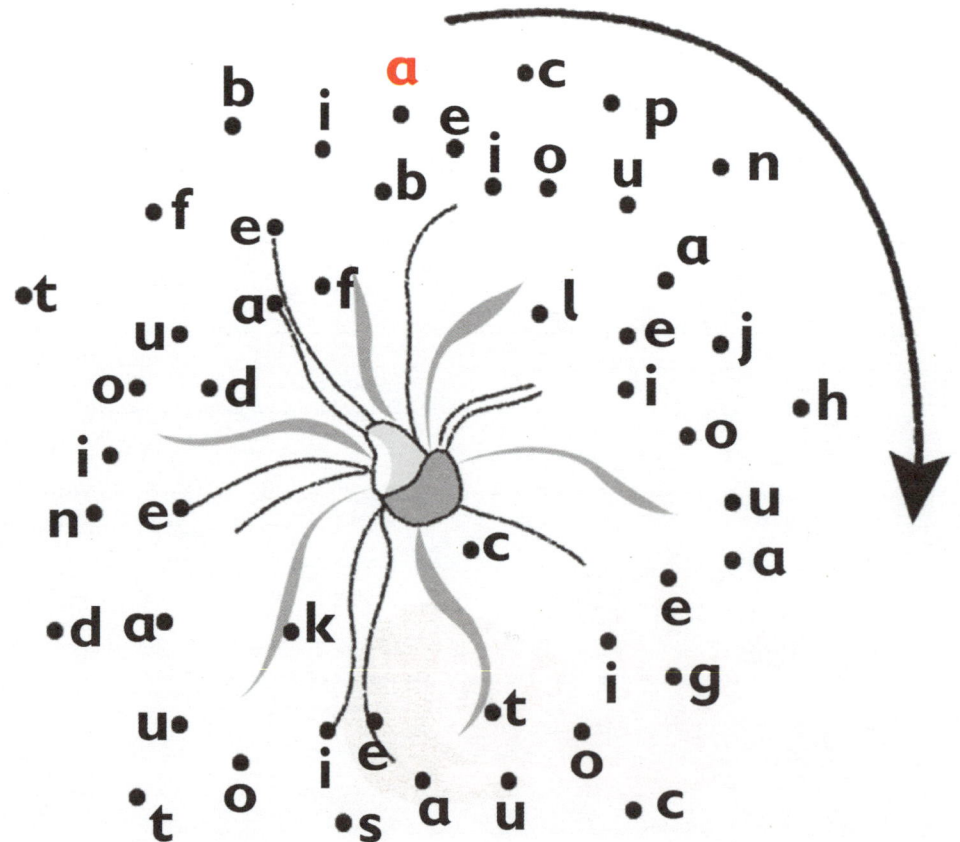

5 marks

② Start at the red **a**. Get to the red **e** by travelling only through squares that contain **vowels**. You cannot move diagonally.

a	e	d	g	y	l	b	p
f	o	m	v	t	t	c	k
w	u	i	y	l	n	m	y
c	v	i	s	s	c	d	n
o	i	a	d	a	e	o	t
i	j	q	v	i	g	i	k
u	a	i	x	u	v	u	a
r	p	i	o	e	r	q	e

5 marks

Challenge 3

① Circle the odd one out in each set of letters.

a) a t o   b) b p h n u   c) e o i s   d) a b c d

4 marks

② Draw lines to match the lowercase **vowels** to their uppercase partners.

 a   e   i   o   u

 I    O    E    U    A

5 marks

③ Write the uppercase **consonant** next to its lowercase partner.

b	c	d	f	g	h	j
k	l	m	n	p	q	r
s	t	v	w	x	y	z

21 marks

How am I doing?   Total marks: /50

Spelling 63

Dictionaries 1

Challenge 1

Dictionaries can help you check your spelling. The words in a dictionary are listed in alphabetical order. You will need to know how the word starts in order to find it in the dictionary. Here is the alphabet to help you.

abcdefghijklmnopqrstuvwxyz

1. Put these words in **alphabetical order**.

   | usually | angrily | mixture | orange | unkind |

   a) ....

   b) ....

   c) ....

   d) ....

   e) ....

   5 marks

2. Use a **dictionary** to find **three** words beginning with the letters **abs**. Write the words you find and the page number you find them on.

Word	Page
....	....
....	....
....	....

   3 marks

3. Now find **three** words beginning with the letters **del**. Write the words you find and the page number you find them on.

Word	Page
....	....
....	....
....	....

   3 marks

Challenge 2

1 Use a **dictionary** to check the spelling of these words. Tick the ones that are **correct**.

gardening ☐   prefer ☐   forgoten ☐

begin ☐   begining ☐   limited ☐

4 marks

2 These words are spelled **incorrectly**. Use a **dictionary** to help you write them correctly on the lines below.

finaly   missbehave   informacion

....

3 marks

Challenge 3

1 Some of the words in the paragraph below are spelled **incorrectly**. Use a **dictionary** to help you check the spellings. Circle the incorrect spellings, then write them correctly on the lines below.

Have you ever wished you could make your chores dissapear with just a snap of your fingers? That would probably be everyone's favrit trick! But instead, we can lurn how to make them fun. For example, try turning cleaning your room into a race to see how much you can tidy in just one minit. Soon enuff, you might find yourself laughing as you put toys away, and before you know it, everything is done!

a) .... b) ....

c) .... d) ....

e) .... f) ....

12 marks

How am I doing?   Total marks: ☐ / 30

Dictionaries 2

Challenge 1

1. Look up each of these words in a **dictionary**. Draw a line to match each word to its meaning.

nocturnal	a 2-D shape with six straight sides
hexagon	extremely large
easel	a large amount of something
autobiography	active at night
abundance	an upright frame to hold a picture that someone is painting
colossal	a book about a person's own life

6 marks

Challenge 2

1. Use a **dictionary** to find the meaning of the words below. Write the definition of each word.

a) amateur ....

....

b) vain ....
....

c) prepare ....
....

d) character ....
....

e) adapt ....
....

f) obstruct ....
....

6 marks

Challenge 3

1. Write your own definitions for the words below. Try to give as much detail as possible.

   a) book ....
   ....

   b) chair ....
   ....

   c) bus ....
   ....

3 marks

2. Find the definitions of the words above in a **dictionary**. Write the definitions below and then compare them to your own.

   a) book ....

   b) chair ....

   c) bus ....

3 marks

How am I doing?   Total marks: /18

Spelling

Progress test 2

1. Write a **homophone** for each of these words.

   a) fare ....

   b) grate ....

   c) plane ....

   d) bear ....

   e) mane ....

   f) knight ....

   g) meat ....

   h) reign ....

8 marks

2. This wordsearch contains words with French, Greek and Latin origins. Find the **seven** words in the box.

chalet
mosque
muscle
scent
school
stomach
tongue

s	m	o	s	k	v	u	r
t	s	c	h	o	o	l	k
o	j	c	x	d	e	a	b
m	c	d	e	z	l	m	z
a	x	t	o	n	g	u	e
c	h	a	l	e	t	s	i
h	u	r	q	o	o	c	g
w	e	e	f	y	t	l	p
i	m	o	s	q	u	e	n

7 marks

68

3. Circle the correct spelling of the words below.

   a) grabed / **grabbed**   b) swimming / swimming

   c) **regretted** / regreted   d) driping / **dripping**

   4 marks

4. Add the correct **prefixes** to the words below.

   un-   in-   dis-   mis-

   a) ....understood   b) ....happy

   c) ....honest   d) ....complete

   4 marks

5. Place these words in the correct columns.

   kind   open   cry   some

   tick   apple   fork   rhythm

0 vowels	1 vowel	2 vowels

   8 marks

6. Circle the words that use the **suffix -ous** correctly.

   hideous   joinous   bestous

   nervous   fantastous   gracious

   3 marks

Progress test 2   69

7. Find **five** words that begin with the letters **tre-** in a **dictionary**. Write them on the lines in alphabetical order.

a) ....

b) ....

c) ....

d) ....

e) ....

8. Correct the spelling of each **contraction**.

a) carn't ....

b) do'nt ....

c) wont' ....

9. Add the **prefix il-** or **im-** to each of the words below.

il   im

a) ....patient

b) ....legal

c) ....mature

d) ....legible

e) ....possible

10. Write a **verb** in each of the boxes below. Then write a sentence containing each verb.

a) [   ] ....

....

b) ☐ ....
....

c) ☐ ....
....

3 marks

11. Find the meanings of these words in a **dictionary**. Write a definition for each word.

a) **tremendous** ▶ ....
....

b) **hysterical** ▶ ....
....

c) **regret** ▶ ....
....

3 marks

12. Read each sentence. Draw a line to the term that matches the underlined word.

The flowers grew <u>because</u> Betty had watered them.	**adverb**
I closed the door <u>quietly</u> behind me.	**preposition**
Arthur put the letters <u>through</u> the letter box.	**conjunction**
<u>April</u> is the rainiest month.	**proper noun**

4 marks

How am I doing?   Total marks: ☐ /57

Progress test 2   71

Fact retrieval 1

Read the passage and answer the questions.

The Roman Empire

Approximately 2000 years ago, the city of Rome was at the centre of the Roman Empire, which ruled more than 45 million people. Its army was the most powerful in the world and conquered many parts of Europe, North Africa and Asia.

At this time, there were more than a million people living in Rome. Rome was a bustling place to live and people spent much of their free time attending gladiator fights. However, with so many people living in just one city, Rome was also dirty and dangerous.

Challenge 1

1 Fill in the gaps.

a) .... 2000 years ago, Rome was at the centre of the Roman Empire.

b) This Empire ruled ....

c) Its army was the most .... in the world.

d) It conquered many parts of ...., ... and Asia.

e) More than .... people lived in Rome.

f) Rome was a .... place.

g) People living in Rome attended .... fights.

h) Rome was also dirty and ....

9 marks

Challenge 2

1 Read the extract again, then answer the questions. Answer in full sentences.

a) How many years ago was the city of Rome at the centre of the Roman Empire? ....

....

....

b) How many people did the Roman Empire rule? ....

....

c) The Roman Empire conquered many parts of which three continents? ....

....

....

d) What did the people of Rome do for entertainment?

....

....

4 marks

Challenge 3

1 Draw a line to match each word to its correct meaning.

powerful	about
approximately	going to
attending	strong, hard to defeat
conquered	busy, lively
bustling	overcame and took control

5 marks

How am I doing?   Total marks: ▢ /18

Reading – Comprehension

Fact retrieval 2

Read this extract from *Alice in Wonderland* and then answer the questions.

Either the well was very deep, or she fell very slowly, for she had plenty of time as she went down to look about her, and to wonder what was going to happen next. First, she tried to look down and make out what she was coming to, but it was too dark to see anything; then she looked at the sides of the well, and noticed that they were filled with cupboards and book-shelves; here and there she saw maps and pictures hung upon pegs. She took down a jar from one of the shelves as she passed: it was labelled 'ORANGE MARMALADE' but to her great disappointment it was empty.

Suddenly she came upon a little three-legged table, all made of solid glass: there was nothing on it but a tiny golden key, and Alice's first idea was that this might belong to one of the doors of the hall; but, alas! Either the locks were too large, or the key was too small, but at any rate it would not open any of them. However, on the second time round, she came upon a low curtain she had not noticed before, and behind it was a little door about fifteen inches high: she tried the little golden key in the lock, and to her great delight it fitted!

Alice opened the door and found that it led into a small passage, not much larger than a rat-hole: she knelt down and looked along the passage into the loveliest garden you ever saw. How she longed to get out of that dark hall, and wander about among those beds of bright flowers and those cool fountains, but she could not even get her head through the doorway.

Challenge 1

1. Fill in the gaps.

   a) The well was very ....

   b) She had plenty of .... as she went down.

   c) First, she tried to ....

   d) But it was too .... to see anything.

   e) She took a jar that was labelled .... but to her disappointment it was empty.

5 marks

74

Challenge 2

1. Answer these questions.

   a) How many legs did the table that Alice found have?

   ....

   b) What was the table made from?

   ....

   c) What was the only thing on the table?

   ....

   d) What was Alice's first idea?

   ....

   e) How tall was the little door?

   ....

5 marks

Challenge 3

1. Answer these questions.

   a) Write two adjectives that are used in the text to describe the passage and hall.

   .... and ....

   b) Copy the text that tells you how small the passage is.

   ....

   c) Copy the text that tells you Alice wanted to escape.

   ....

   ....

   d) Copy the text that shows Alice could not fit.

   ....

   ....

4 marks

How am I doing?   Total marks: / 14

Traditional tales 1

Challenge 1

1. Read each clue and write the name of the story it describes.

   a) A little girl visits her grandma but finds that she has been eaten by a wolf. The wolf dresses up as her grandma but she notices the wolf's big eyes, ears and teeth! She is saved by a woodcutter.

   ....

   b) A poor girl, who lives with her horrid sisters, is granted a wish by her fairy godmother. She goes to a party where she meets a prince. He finds her after she leaves her glass slipper behind.

   ....

   c) A young boy sells his prize cow for a handful of magic beans. He visits a castle in the clouds where he meets a giant. He steals the giant's magic goose and escapes just in time!

   ....

3 marks

Challenge 2

1. Complete the table to show the hero / heroine and villain in each of these **traditional tales**.

Traditional tale	Hero / Heroine	Villain(s)
a) Jack and the Beanstalk		
b) Cinderella		Ugly Sisters
c) The Three Little Pigs		
d) Little Red Riding Hood	Woodcutter	
e) Hansel and Gretel		

8 marks

Challenge 3

1. Complete the planning grid for the story of *Little Red Riding Hood*.

	Cinderella	**Little Red Riding Hood**
a) Settings	The ugly sisters' cottage in the forest. The prince's ballroom in the castle.	
b) Good characters	Cinderella, Fairy Godmother, Prince Charming, Buttons	
c) Evil / bad characters	Ugly Sisters	
d) Challenges / problems	Cinderella is forbidden to go to the ball. She doesn't have any clothes to wear and can't get to the ball. The prince can't find Cinderella after the ball.	
e) Solution	The fairy godmother gives her a dress, and turns a pumpkin into a carriage and some mice into horses. The prince searches the town for the owner of the glass slipper.	
f) Ending	The prince finds Cinderella and they live happily ever after.	

6 marks

How am I doing?   Total marks: ☐ /17

Traditional tales 2

Challenge 1

1. Circle the characters that you would expect to see in a **traditional tale**.

wolf	wicked stepmother	princess	robot
clown	shark	fairy godmother	snowman

   4 marks

2. Choose the best word to describe each character. Draw a line to match each character to the description.

   a) Fairy Godmother — cunning

   b) Big Bad Wolf — brave

   c) Princess — magical

   d) Woodcutter — selfish

   e) Ugly Sister — kind-hearted

   5 marks

Challenge 2

1. Use these **adjectives** to complete the table below.

   strong   courageous   sly   dishonest   greedy
   caring   rude   untrustworthy   kind   generous

Heroes / Heroines	Villains

   10 marks

78

② Create a **word web** to describe the characters below.
Use a **thesaurus** to help you find some exciting adjectives.

Princess

Troll

10 marks

Challenge 3

① Read the passage below, then answer the questions.

> The young princess was very beautiful and charming, but above all she was extremely kind. She would always smile and talk happily with the people of the town, who all loved her dearly. She lived with her mother and father (the king and queen) in a huge castle where she would spend her days tending to her animals and taking care of her sick aunt. The young princess was also very generous and she would often give money and food to help the poor town folk.

a) Is the princess a good character or an evil character? ....

1 mark

b) Give **three** examples from the text to show how you know.

....
....
....

3 marks

How am I doing?   Total marks: /33

Reading – Comprehension

Poetry

Read the poem *Daddy Fell into the Pond* by Alfred Noyes out loud. Then answer the questions in Challenges 1–3.

Everyone grumbled. The sky was grey.
We had nothing to do and nothing to say.
We were nearing the end of a dismal day,
And there seemed to be nothing beyond,
THEN
Daddy fell into the pond!

And everyone's face grew merry and bright,
And Timothy danced for sheer delight.
"Give me the camera, quick, oh quick!
He's crawling out of the duckweed!"
Click!

Then the gardener suddenly slapped his knee,
And doubled up, shaking silently,
And the ducks all quacked as if they were daft,
And it sounded as if the old drake laughed.
Oh, there wasn't a thing that didn't respond.
WHEN
Daddy fell into the pond!

Challenge 1

1 Fill in the gaps to complete parts of the poem.

   a) .... grumbled. The sky was grey.

   b) And everyone's face grew .... and ....

   c) "He's crawling out of the ....!"

   4 marks

2 Write **two** pairs of words from the poem that rhyme.

   a) .... and ....

   b) .... and ....

2 marks

80

Challenge 2

1. Read the word in each box. Write another word that means the same next to each word.

   a) grumbled ....

   b) dismal ....

   c) merry ....

   d) laughed ....

   4 marks

2. Answer the questions below.

   a) What **onomatopoeic word** tells the reader that Timothy has taken a picture of Daddy?

   ....

   b) What is the repeated phrase in the poem?

   ....

   2 marks

Challenge 3

1. Answer the questions below in full sentences.

   a) Who do you think Timothy is? Explain your answer.

   ....

   b) Why is the gardener described as 'shaking silently'?

   ....

   c) How did the poem make you feel? Explain your answer.

   ....

   3 marks

How am I doing?   Total marks: ☐ /15

Writer's purpose

Challenge 1

1. Tick each sentence below to show if the writer is stating a **fact** or **describing something** (description).

	Fact	Description
a) The sun shone brightly in the sky like an orange ball.		
b) I went bowling yesterday.		
c) About 1 in 10 people are vegetarian.		
d) She meandered through the crowds like a snake stalking its prey.		

4 marks

2. Read the sentences below. Draw a line to match each sentence to the purpose of writing.

a) Come to Zak's fun fair. You'll have the time of your life!

b) The supermarket opens daily from 7 am until 10 pm.

c) With a hood covering his face, a mysterious figure emerged from the dark shadows.

to inform

to entertain

to persuade

3 marks

Challenge 2

1. Read each sentence and write whether its purpose is to **inform**, **entertain** or **persuade**.

a) Bananas are high in fibre but also very high in natural sugars. ....

b) The new superhero film is fantastic – you should definitely see it.

....

82

c) The raging sea thrashed against the jagged cliffs, roaring as it swelled up. ....

d) There are 339 different breeds of dogs. ....

e) In the sky, the clouds danced playfully. ....

f) Recycle your rubbish if you want to help protect our planet.
....

6 marks

Challenge 3

1) Use the information in the advert below to answer the questions.

> Would you like to visit another planet?
>
> The all-new and exciting trip on the Space Shuttle 12 will take you on a once-in-a-lifetime visit to a planet of your choice. Whether it be Mars, Jupiter or Pluto, this experience is sure to be out of this world!
>
> Only £5 600 000 per person
>
> For all enquiries, please contact 01125 598745.

a) What is the purpose of the advert? ....
....

b) Why has the writer used the phrase 'once-in-a-lifetime'?
....

c) Why has the writer started the advert with a question?
....

d) Why has the writer used the phrase 'out of this world'?
....

4 marks

How am I doing?   　　Total marks: ☐ /17

Reading – Comprehension　　83

Making predictions

Challenge 1

1. Read the extract below and then tick the events that you think could happen next.

> Arya was stirring the cake mixture in a big bowl when she noticed the recipe book had flipped to a different page. She stopped and frowned.
>
> "Wait, did I already add the sugar?" she wondered out loud. Her little brother, Kian, was sitting at the table, licking a spoon covered in chocolate. Arya glanced at the sugar jar on the counter and bit her lip, unsure of what to do next.

Arya tastes the mixture to check if it's sweet enough.

The mixing bowl starts talking and tells Arya what to do.

Kian might remember seeing her add the sugar earlier.

Arya decides to add the sugar anyway, just in case.

Kian turns into a giant cupcake.

3 marks

Challenge 2

1. Read these scenarios and **predict** what might happen next.

a) Patrick and Alejandro were excited about building sandcastles at the beach. As they began to set up their chairs, Patrick looked up and saw a big grey cloud.

What could happen next?

....

....

84

b) Mrs Morris was driving to work. With lots on her mind, she took her eyes off the road for just a second.

What could happen next?

....

....

2 marks

Challenge 3

1. Read the extract below. **Predict** what may happen next. Write your prediction on the lines below.

> Maui picked up the brush and began to sweep the leaves as Mum had asked her.
>
> "You can go and get an ice cream once you have finished," Maui's mum had told her. Ten minutes passed and she didn't seem to be getting anywhere with all the leaves. In the distance, Maui heard a faint noise that grew louder and louder.
>
> "Oh no, the ice-cream van," she thought. Maui glanced back at the house where Mum was ironing in the front room. "Maybe she won't mind if I go and get my ice cream first and then finish the garden," Maui thought.

....

....

....

2 marks

How am I doing?

Total marks: / 7

Reading – Comprehension   85

Inference 1

Challenge 1

1 Use the picture below to help you answer the questions.

a) Is it 11.05 in the morning or in the evening?

....

b) How do you know? ....

....

c) How many people are going to have a glass of water? ....

....

d) How do you know? ....

....

4 marks

Challenge 2

1 Write how the boy is feeling in each picture.

a) 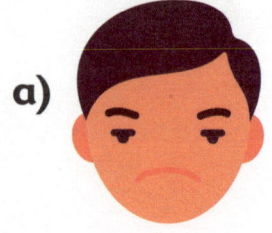   b)    c)

....

3 marks

Challenge 3

1 Underline the **verbs** in each sentence below.

   a) Alyssa sat in the corner, tears rolling down her face.

   b) Jemma's face turned redder and redder as she clenched her fists together.

   c) Jumping up and down, Jonah giggled with glee.

   d) Aaron ripped his work into lots of pieces and marched out of the room.

   e) With his arms folded, a scowl crossed the headteacher's face.

   10 marks

2 Write a sentence to show how each character in the sentences above was feeling.

   a) **Alyssa** ....

   ....

   b) **Jemma** ....

   ....

   c) **Jonah** ....

   ....

   d) **Aaron** ....

   ....

   e) **The headteacher** ....

   ....

   5 marks

How am I doing?   Total marks: ___ /22

Reading – Comprehension   87

Inference 2

Challenge 1

1 Read the clue in the speech bubble, then tick the correct answer.

a) What time of day is it?

The sun is in my eyes!   morning ☐   night ☐

b) How is the person feeling?

Please will you pass my coat.   too hot ☐   too cold ☐

c) What does the person want to do?

I'm thirsty.   eat something ☐   drink something ☐

3 marks

Challenge 2

1 Draw a line to match the underlined word to its meaning.

a) The street was <u>bustling</u> with lots of tourists.   —   hungry

b) Darkness <u>engulfed</u> the town, hiding it from view.   —   not moving

c) The boys were <u>ravenous</u>. They hadn't eaten since lunchtime.   —   busy

d) The cars were <u>stationary</u> in a traffic jam.   —   covered completely

4 marks

2. Circle the words in each sentence that suggest it is sunny weather.

   a) Around him, almost everyone had shorts on.

   b) The sun sizzled in the sky.

   c) Puddles that had been there before had now dried up.

Challenge 3

1. Read the passage below. Underline any words or phrases that give the idea that the town was busy.

   > Crowds packed the streets. There were tourists everywhere. Every shop was crowded and there was barely space for anyone to fit through the doors. Visitors meandered, slowly moving across the square. They added to the volume of people in the streets and created a human traffic jam. There was no shelter from the sun today. Every inch of shade was occupied.

Progress test 3

1. Circle the stories that are **traditional tales**.

   Little Red Riding Hood

   Hansel and Gretel

   Harry Potter

   The Gruffalo

   Jack and the Beanstalk

   The BFG

   3 marks

2. Write a sentence for each word to show its meaning.

   a) **impolite** ....
   ....

   b) **nervously** ....
   ....

   c) **texture** ....
   ....

   3 marks

3. Write the correct spelling on the line next to each word.

   a) **serios** ....

   b) **posible** ....

   c) **deside** ....

   3 marks

Read the extract from *The Tales of Peter Rabbit* by Beatrix Potter. Then answer questions 4–9.

> Once upon a time there were four little rabbits, and their names were Flopsy, Mopsy, Cotton-tail and Peter. They lived with their mother in a sand-bank, underneath the root of a very big fir tree.
>
> "Now, my dears," said old Mrs Rabbit one morning, "you may go into the fields or down the lane, but don't go into Mr McGregor's garden: your father had an accident there; he was put in a pie by Mrs McGregor. Now run along, and don't get into mischief. I am going out."
>
> Flopsy, Mopsy, and Cotton-tail, who were good little bunnies, went down the lane to gather blackberries.
>
> But Peter, who was very naughty, ran straight away to Mr McGregor's garden, and squeezed under the gate!
>
> First, he ate some lettuces and some French beans; and then he ate some radishes.
>
> And then, feeling rather sick, he went to look for some parsley.
>
> But round the end of a cucumber frame, whom should he meet but Mr McGregor!
>
> Mr McGregor was on his hands and knees planting out young cabbages, but he jumped up and ran after Peter, waving a rake and calling out, "Stop thief."
>
> Peter was most dreadfully frightened; he rushed all over the garden, for he had forgotten the way back to the gate.

4. Circle the correct answer from the choices below each question.

   a) This extract is…

   fiction   non-fiction

Progress test 3   91

b) The four young rabbits were called Flopsy, Mopsy, Cotton-tail and...

- Mr McGregor
- Roger
- Mrs Rabbit
- Peter

c) When in Mr McGregor's garden, Mr Rabbit had an accident and...

- hurt his leg
- was put in a pie by Mrs McGregor
- got stuck in a bush

d) Flopsy, Mopsy and Cotton-tail went to look for...

- apples
- raspberries
- blackberries
- blueberries

e) Peter ate some .... and .... first.

- French beans
- radishes
- parsley
- lettuces

6 marks

5. Draw a line to match the words from the extract to the correct term.

- verb — underneath
- common noun — radishes
- proper noun — planting
- preposition — Mopsy

4 marks

92

6. Answer the following questions in full sentences. Remember to read the extract again to help.

   a) Where did Peter meet Mr McGregor?

   ....

   b) What did Mr McGregor shout at Peter?

   ....

   c) How did Mr McGregor feel when he saw Peter?

   ....

   d) How did Peter feel when he could not remember the way back to the gate?

   ....

   4 marks

7. Explain what you think will happen to Peter in the next part of the story.

   ....

   1 mark

8. Read the sentence below. Why does the author use an **exclamation mark** here?

   > But round the end of a cucumber frame, whom should he meet but Mr McGregor!

   ....

   1 mark

9. Add the correct punctuation to each sentence below to show **speech**.

   a) Now, my dears, said old Mrs Rabbit.

   b) Mr McGregor called out, Stop thief!

   2 marks

How am I doing?

Total marks: ___ / 27

Learning from other writers

Challenge 1

1. Look at each word shown in **red**. Write **adjective**, **verb** or **noun** to say what type of word it is.

   a) Amrit **fell** over the huge brown log. ....

   b) The **wide** river flowed gently past the town. ....

   c) The children saw jugglers and acrobats at the **circus**. ....

   d) Mum wanted Chloe to **take** out the rubbish and clean her bedroom. ....

   e) The children went on a school trip to see a **play** at the theatre. ....

   5 marks

Challenge 2

1. Circle all of the **adjectives** in the sentences below.

   a) The enormous tree towered over the forest.

   b) Three of the naughty puppies chewed the man's slipper.

   c) The beautiful woman was sitting quietly by the waterfall.

   d) Behind the empty park was a huge field.

   e) Jane took her new fish tank home and put it in her bedroom.

   f) The sky was dark, black and stormy.

   6 marks

2. Make each sentence more effective by changing the **adjectives**. Write each new improved sentence on the lines below.

   a) The **big** troll lived under the bridge.

   ....

   ....

94

b) Kaylee loved her **nice** jewellery box.

....

....

c) The **mad** wolf chased the people out of the town.

....

....

d) Calum watched the player score a **good** goal.

....

....

e) The **small** children were terrified by the **scary** ghost story.

....

....

5 marks

Challenge 3

1) Create your own word bank about the seaside using adjective-noun-verb combinations. An example has been done for you.

Adjective	Noun	Verb
e.g. cold	ice cream	melted
a)		
b)		
c)		

9 marks

2) Use your word bank to help you write an exciting description of the seaside. Continue your answer on a separate piece of paper if needed.

....

....

....

5 marks

How am I doing?   Total marks: ☐ /30

Writing – Composition

Sentence structure

Challenge 1

1 Tick each complete sentence below.

She ran towards the door. ☐   It swayed. ☐

As the sun set. ☐   There was silence. ☐

Beyond the hills. ☐   Purple flowers. ☐

3 marks

2 Tick to show whether each of the groups of words below is a **sentence** or a **phrase**. An example has been done for you.

		Sentence	Phrase
e.g.	In the box		✓
a)	The bird soared high in the sky.		
b)	Quietly, the rabbit retreated.		
c)	From the darkness		
d)	It emerged.		
e)	Above the trees		

5 marks

Challenge 2

1 Read the words in each box. Match each box to the correct term.

because I was hungry	a phrase
to the swimming pool	a question
My house is in London.	an exclamation
How many pizzas do we need?	a noun phrase
Wow, a hot air balloon!	a clause
that sweet little mouse	a statement

6 marks

96

Challenge 3

1. Choose a suitable ending from the boxes to finish each sentence. Complete the sentence on the line.

| a light suddenly appeared. | a mysterious figure emerged. | he unwrapped the gift. |

| the teacher ended the lesson. | they headed for home. |  |

a) Out of the darkness, ...

b) As the sun began to set, ...

c) When the bell rang, ...

d) From behind the tree, ...

e) With a smile on his face, ...

5 marks

2. Complete the sentences below. Remember to punctuate the sentences correctly.

a) With her hair blowing in the wind, she ....
....

b) As the clock struck midnight, ...

c) All of a sudden, ...

d) Beyond the horizon, ...

e) High above, ...

5 marks

How am I doing?   Total marks: /24

Writing – Composition 97

Fronted adverbials

Challenge 1

1. Draw a line to match each **fronted adverbial** to a sentence on the right.

> Adverbials at the start of a sentence are called **fronted adverbials**. They can tell the reader **when** something happens.

a) On Monday,

b) When my alarm went off,

c) Before lunch,

d) After Art class,

e) At 8 o'clock in the evening,

I jumped out of bed.

I started a new week at school.

I went to bed.

I washed my hands.

I got my things for home time.

5 marks

2. Add the **comma** in the correct place after each **fronted adverbial** below.

> Fronted adverbials need to be punctuated with a **comma** after the phrase. For example: Yesterday, I fell over and hurt my knee.

a) During the night the owls left their nests to hunt.

b) Aged four I went on my first holiday abroad.

c) On Tuesdays I have my saxophone lesson at school.

d) At 3.15 pm the bell rang to go home.

e) After my bath I got ready for bed.

5 marks

98

Challenge 2

1. Use the picture to complete the sentence using a **fronted adverbial**. Remember to punctuate each sentence with a comma.

   a)  After .... I brushed my teeth.

   b)  At .... I ate my lunch.

   c)  Before .... I returned home.

   d)  On .... I played football.

   4 marks

2. Underline the **fronted adverbial** in each sentence.

   a) After dinner, I played on the computer.

   b) In an instant, the wood fell quiet.

   c) With the saddle on her horse, Lucy was ready to go riding.

   3 marks

Challenge 3

1. Create your own **fronted adverbials** to show **when** things happen. Choose from the words below to start each sentence.

   | After | When | As | At | On |

   a) .... I quickly ran inside.

   b) .... I have PE at school.

   c) .... I woke up.

   d) .... I will go on holiday.

4 marks

How am I doing?

Total marks: ____ /21

Writing – Composition 99

Organising non-fiction writing

Challenge 1

1. Draw a line to join each **subheading** from a non-fiction report about a robin to information that would be included in it.

Introduction	What a robin is and what the report will tell the reader
Appearance	What a robin eats
Diet	A summary of the main points
Habitat	What a robin looks like
Conclusion	Where a robin lives

5 marks

Challenge 2

1. Read the information in the **paragraph** below. Write a **subheading** for the paragraph.

Guinea pigs are rodents that originated from the deserts of South America. There are many breeds of guinea pig and all have a slightly different appearance. Guinea pigs are a very common pet because they are playful and fairly easy to look after. This report will tell you all about guinea pigs, including their appearance, what they eat, where they live in the wild and how to look after them.

Subheading ....

1 mark

Challenge 3

1. Write **five** things that you would include in a **paragraph** about your school uniform: what it looks like, why you have it, how much it cost, etc.

   a) ....

   b) ....

   c) ....

   d) ....

   e) ....

   5 marks

2. Use your ideas above to create a **paragraph** about your school uniform. Add the name of your school to the subheading.

   > Think about the order of sentences:
   >
   > Which sentence will you start with?
   >
   > How will you end your paragraph?

   School uniform at _____

   ....
   ....
   ....
   ....
   ....
   ....
   ....
   ....

   5 marks

How am I doing?   Total marks: ____ / 16

Organising fiction writing

Challenge 1

1. What are the **three** main parts of a story? Write them below.

   a) ....

   b) ....

   c) ....

   3 marks

2. Match each part of a story to what is included in that section.

   a) **Beginning** — There is a problem or something changes in the story.

   b) **Middle** — The problem is solved.

   c) **End** — The setting and the main characters are introduced.

   3 marks

Challenge 2

1. Use the story mountain to plot the main events of the story *The Three Little Pigs*.

   Beginning
   ....
   ....
   ....

   Middle
   ....
   ....
   ....
   ....

   End
   ....
   ....
   ....

   3 marks

2. Use the planning grid to plan your own story.

Beginning – setting and characters	
Middle – a problem occurs	
Ending – the problem is solved	

6 marks

Challenge 3

1. Use your planning grid to help you write your own story. Continue your answer on a separate piece of paper if needed.

....
....
....
....
....
....
....
....

10 marks

How am I doing? 😐 🙂 😊   Total marks: /25

Writing – Composition

Character and setting description

Your challenge is to create a scary story. You will need to think carefully about the setting for your story and the main character. These pages will help you to design your setting and your character, and write about them.

Challenge 1

1. Draw a picture of your spooky **setting** and main **character**.

   - Where is your spooky setting? A graveyard, a deserted house or somewhere else?

   - What will the things in your picture look like? Will they be unusual? Will they be well kept or old and falling apart?

   - What will the weather be like? Dark? Stormy? Windy? Calm?

   - Which colours will you use? Will they be bright or dark colours?

   - Who is in your setting? Are they good or evil? A hero / heroine or a villain?

5 marks

Challenge 2

1. Fill the diagrams below with **adjectives** to describe your **setting** and main **character**. Use a thesaurus to help you.

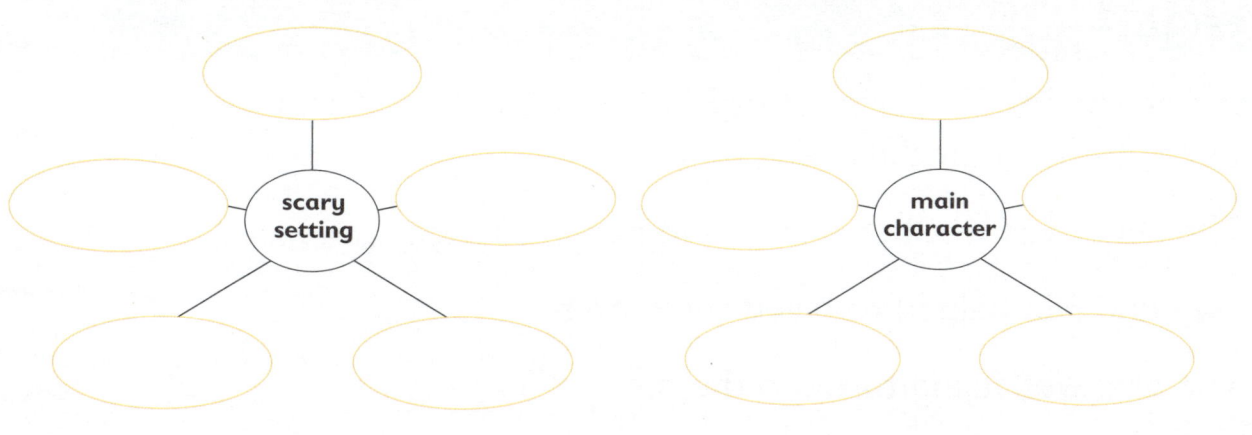

10 marks

Challenge 3

1. Use your **picture** and your **adjectives** to write some sentences to describe your **setting** and main **character**.

....
....
....
....
....
....
....
....
....

5 marks

How am I doing?   　　Total marks: ▢ / 20

Proofreading

Challenge 1

1. Underline the **incorrect spelling** in each sentence. Write the **correct spelling** on the line.

   a) The road was wet becouse it had been raining. ....

   b) Ivan and Ella helped to billed the model. ....

   c) The bird wos flying through the air. ....

   6 marks

2. Read each sentence. Check the punctuation and spelling, then tick or cross the appropriate box. The first one has been done for you.

	Punctuation	Spelling
a) The bird sat <u>quitly</u> on the fence.	✓	✗
b) Ive read all of the books on my shelf.		
c) The cat ran threw the open window.		
d) Mei saw birds fish and snakes in the pet shop		
e) I couldnt carry the heavey shopping.		

   4 marks

Challenge 2

1. Tick the boxes to show the **punctuation** that is missing from each sentence.

	'	.	,
a) The school holidays last for seven weeks			
b) We ate peas carrots and potatoes for lunch.			
c) Our dog Alvin didnt want to go for a walk.			
d) Weve been waiting a long time for the bus			

   4 marks

2 Correct the **punctuation** and **grammar**, then rewrite the sentences.

a) anil didn't want to go to the cinema on monday

....

b) the family went to paris on their holidays

....

c) the rain in january was worse than in december

....

d) elijah and chantal couldnt find their car keys in the house

....

....

4 marks

Challenge 3

1 Read the paragraph below carefully. Correct the **spelling**, **punctuation** and **grammar**.

smudge was a norty little puppy who loved getting into trouble. One day, he would'nt stop digging in Dads garden, even though he was told not to. Smudge thort it was the perfect place to hide his favourite bone, but when Dad saw the mess, he weren't happy! Smudge tryed to look innocent, but their was mud grass and daisies all over his nose and paws. everyone laughed, and even Dad had to smile – smudge allways found a way to make things fun

13 marks

How am I doing?   Total marks: [ ] / 31

Writing – Composition 107

Progress test 4

1. Tick the information that could be in a report about Egypt.

   a) Egyptians built pyramids for their kings. ☐

   b) Much of Egypt is desert. ☐

   c) The weather in Spain is mostly warm. ☐

   d) Cocoa beans are grown in South America. ☐

   e) The capital of Egypt is Cairo. ☐

   3 marks

GPS 2. **Proofread** the sentences for **spelling**, **grammar** and **punctuation**. Underline any errors and rewrite the sentences.

   a) They was happy

   ....

   b) mum didnt like my favrit rollercoaster ride.

   ....

   c) On tuesdays we go to karate.

   ....

   d) James and bill are coming to the park They are coming in dads car.

   ....

e) Jill have danced in five shows in Febuary.

....

3. Underline the **adjective** in each sentence below.

a) The green grass danced in the wind.

b) The dark forest loomed in the distance.

c) The pirate had a multi-coloured parrot.

d) She ran towards the empty house.

e) I heard the rusty gate creak in the wind.

4. Use ambitious **adjectives** to describe the **character** below.

....

....

5. Describe the **setting** for an adventure in a jungle. What interesting **adjectives** will you use? What can you see and hear?

- ....
- ....
- ....
- ....
- ....
- ....

13 marks

5 marks

6 marks

7 marks

Progress test 4

6. Circle the **adjective** that makes each **noun phrase** more interesting.

  a) **The big / colossal waterfall** crashed onto **the wet / sodden rocks**.

  b) **Ten minuscule / small mice** scuttled past **the scared / petrified shopkeeper**.

  c) **Their hot / scorching teas** steamed in **the icy / cool air**.

6 marks

7. Write sentences starting with each phrase below.

  a) In the distance, ...

  ....

  b) Without a sound, ...

  ....

  c) From across the room, ...

  ....

3 marks

8. Complete each sentence with a **fronted adverbial** to show when the action happens.

  a) ...., the moon rose in the sky.

  b) ...., the children went home exhausted.

  c) ...., we visited the beach.

  d) ...., the dog fell asleep by the fire.

4 marks

9. Change the adjectives below into **adverbs**.

  a) quiet ....

  b) safe ....

  c) rapid ....

  d) sudden ....

4 marks

10. Replace the underlined **verbs** and **adjectives** in the paragraph with more exciting options. The first one has been done for you.

The ~~tall~~ *towering* walls of the ancient castle loomed overhead as Leo walked .... cautiously across the crumbling stone bridge, the wind blowing .... around him. He ran his fingers over the gold .... medallion in his pocket. He had to return it to the good .... king. Suddenly, a loud clang echoed behind him, and he jumped, turning .... around to see the rusty portcullis slamming shut. He looked .... up towards the battlements and froze. A dark .... figure stood there, pointing directly at him. Before he could decide whether to run .... away or hide, the ground beneath him began to shake.

8 marks

11. Write the **ending** to the story above. Use **noun phrases**, **verbs** and **adverbials** that will make the reader want to read more. Continue your answer on a separate piece of paper if needed.

....

....

....

....

....

8 marks

How am I doing?

Total marks: ☐ / 67

Answers

For questions worth 1 mark with several answer spaces, all answers should be correct to achieve the mark, unless otherwise indicated.

Pages 4–11

Starter test

1. Answers will vary.
2. a) st**ay**, aw**ay**, cr**ay**on
   b) potat**oes**, tipt**oe**, g**oes**
   c) th**ir**d, tw**ir**l, squ**ir**t, b**ir**thday
3. a) ba**th**, **th**under   b) too**th**, **th**ree
   c) **th**igh, **th**ink, bo**th**
4. a) **gr**ape, ever**gr**een   b) **st**amp, **st**icker, be**st**
   c) rou**nd**, sa**nd**storm
5. a) **wh**ale   b) **ph**otogra**ph**
   c) tele**ph**one   d) **wh**ich
   e) ele**ph**ant   f) **wh**isper
6. The wolf pretends to be Grandma and tricks Little Red Riding Hood. — 2
   Little Red Riding Hood sets off to Grandma's to take her some flowers. — 1
   The woodcutter saves Little Red Riding Hood and Grandma. — 3
7. a) loyal
   b) guiding people who cannot see, helping on farms
   c) regular exercise
8. a) **fl**y   b) **bl**end   c) **spl**ash
9. b) foot + ball = football
   c) rain + bow = rainbow
   d) butter + fly = butterfly
   e) cup + cake = cupcake
10. a) dough — nut → doughnut
    b) farm — house → farmhouse
    c) draw — bridge → drawbridge
    d) bath — room → bathroom
11. Answers will vary, e.g. teabag, blackbird, sunset
12. b) have not = haven't   c) cannot = can't
    d) I am = I'm   e) you are = you're
    f) will not = won't
13. **I'd** really like to go to the funfair on Sunday. Daisy told me that **she'd** like to come too but she **can't** go until after lunch. If I went on my own it **wouldn't** be as much fun, so I think **I'll** wait for her.
14. a)–c) Answers will vary, e.g. I believe that it will rain at the weekend; I could not answer the question that the teacher asked; Out of the corner of my eye, I saw a figure appear.
15. a) enjoy**ment**   b) help**ful**
    c) kind**ness**
16. a) **dis** + **agree** = **disagree**
    b) **re** + **arrange** = **rearrange**
    c) **im** + **patient** = **impatient**
17. a) The wild storm raged through the **night**.
    b) The teacher asked the boys to bring in **their** homework.
    c) We could **hear** the birds singing in the trees.
18. The children were playing with <u>there</u> swords and shields. Ahmad wanted to be the brave <u>night</u> and Priya wanted to be the princess. <u>They're</u> mum could <u>here</u> them shouting and asked them to keep <u>there</u> voices down.
19. a) Why is the sky blue – **?**
    b) The boys walked to the park – **.**
    c) How wonderful – **!**
20. b) England starts with a capital letter because it is the name of a place, which is a proper noun.
    c) January starts with a capital letter because it is the name of a month of the year, which is a proper noun.
21. **O**n **T**hursday**, T**im and **K**ira went for a walk with their dog**, B**illy**. I**t was cold and they had forgotten their hats**,** so they did not stay out for very long**. I**t was **M**arch**,** after all!
22. a) flew   b) ran
    c) drove   d) played
    e) swam
23. Answers will vary.
24. a) I will go outside if it stops raining. ✓
    c) The flowers will bloom if the sun keeps shining. ✓
    d) I will not go to school if I am poorly. ✓
25. James, Wednesday, Cornwall
26. Answers will vary.

Pages 12–13
Challenge 1
1. a) chair b) bus c) apple
   d) window e) slide f) feather
2. a) I sat beneath a <u>tree</u>.
   b) He walked along the <u>river</u>.
   c) Trevor threw the <u>ball</u> very high.

Challenge 2
1. a) <u>Sanjit</u> went bowling with his **friend**, <u>Andrei</u>.
   b) In <u>Scotland</u>, there are lots of wild **deer**.
   c) On <u>Saturday</u>, <u>Beth</u> will visit her **dad**, who lives near the **beach**.
2. a) <u>He</u> went for a walk.
   b) <u>You</u> are my friend.
   c) <u>They</u> wrapped lots of presents.
   d) I gave <u>it</u> to <u>her</u>.
   e) <u>We</u> helped <u>him</u>.

Challenge 3
1. Common nouns: glass, book
   Proper nouns: November, Marcus, Scotland
   Pronouns: we, them, she

Pages 14–15
Challenge 1
1.

a	o	r	u	m	s	a
i	h	s	r	u	n	w	s
p	h	p	f	h	l	d	w
r	c	w	o	d	e	i	i
s	t	o	h	i	k	n	m
e	a	t	w	i	n	t	n
b	w	c	z	l	t	e	v
a	n	s	p	i	k	s	y

Challenge 2
1. a) Tyler <u>jogged</u> home.
   b) Rosina <u>played</u> outside with her friends.
   c) The dogs <u>barked</u> at the squirrels.
   d) I <u>am</u> happy.
   e) Tomorrow, James will <u>go</u> to the cinema.
2. Answers will vary, e.g.
   a) After school, Ali **watched** TV.
   b) Jason **read** a book to his Dad.
   c) Jan **ate** an apple.

Challenge 3
1. The ancient Egyptians <u>lived</u> along the River Nile in Egypt. They <u>grew</u> crops like wheat and barley and <u>ate</u> bread, vegetables and fish. Men and women sometimes <u>wore</u> jewellery to <u>show</u> their status. For fun, they <u>liked</u> board games, <u>danced</u> and <u>made</u> music with harps and flutes. Children <u>played</u> with toys like dolls and balls. The Egyptians <u>built</u> temples, <u>created</u> beautiful art, and <u>honoured</u> their gods with ceremonies and festivals.
   lived, grew, ate, wore, show, liked, danced, made, played, built, created, honoured

Pages 16–17
Challenge 1
1. a) Angus **has swung** the bat.
   b) I **have drunk** all the orange juice.
   c) The dog **has caught** the ball.
   d) Ricardo **has watched** the football game on TV.
   e) Monika **has washed** the dishes in the cottage.
   f) The boys **have dipped** their biscuits in their tea.
   g) The referee **has blown** her whistle too loudly.
   h) My brother and I **have collected** conkers since we were four.

Challenge 2
1. a) The birds **have** sung all day.
   b) She **has** watched television all evening.
   c) We **have** supported our team for five years.
   d) The nurse **has** worked there since she was twenty years old.
   e) The wind **has** blown strongly all day.
   f) The dogs **have** howled all night.
   g) We **have** watched that programme since it started.
   h) They **have** always wanted to visit this museum.
2. a) past ✓ b) present perfect ✓
   c) present perfect ✓ d) past ✓

Challenge 3
1. Answers will vary.
2. a) I **have decorated** / **have been decorating** the house for Mum's birthday.
   b) You **have read** / **have been reading** three books about stars.
   c) She **has played** / **has been playing** the piano since she was six.
   d) They **have scored** three goals since half time.
   e) The sun **has shone** / **has been shining** all day.

Pages 18–19

Challenge 1
1. a) Saskia **bravely** <u>fought</u> the dragon.
   b) Chadi <u>used</u> the scissors **carefully**.
2. a) The tortoise plodded **slowly** back home.
   b) You performed **fantastically** in the school play.
   c) The dog wagged its tail **happily**.

Challenge 2
1. a) **Finally**, he sang his wonderful song.
   b) I **usually** sing in assembly.
   c) **Today**, Lucy wants to sing with the choir.
   d) Rupert **never** sings.
   e) We sang six songs **yesterday**.
2. When it's sunny, ——— outside.
   Sue prefers to eat

   Place your empty plate ——— here.

   I can sleep ——— anywhere.

Challenge 3
1. Answers will vary.

Pages 20–21

Challenge 1
1. a) It was raining **so** I put up my umbrella. ✓
   c) It was a very cold day **yet** the sun was shining. ✓
   d) Mrs Chen liked running **but** she preferred tennis. ✓
2. a) I could use the front door **or** I could use the kitchen door.
   b) His dog loves puddles **but** he hates getting wet.
   c) Max is five years old **and** his sister is ten.

Challenge 2
1. a) Marnie finished her homework **so** she got a gold star.
   b) You might be sick **if** you eat too many sweets.
   c) My mum was angry **because** we broke her vase.
2. I am lucky ——— **because** I got a telescope for my birthday.

   I can see the full moon ——— **when** I use my telescope.

   The stars look so close ——— **yet** they are so far away.

Challenge 3
1. Lions are known as the kings of the jungle **because** they are powerful predators with no natural enemies. They are often portrayed as solitary hunters **although** lions are actually social animals that live in prides. **If** a lion pride works together, they can take down large prey like buffalo or giraffes, providing enough food for everyone. The lionesses are usually responsible for hunting **while** the males often defend the pride. Lions take turns eating **so** even the cubs have a chance to feed.

Pages 22–23

Challenge 1
1. a) I climbed into bed **after** brushing my teeth.
   b) The train pulled up at the station, **then** let the passengers off.
   c) I scratch my dog's tummy **when** she rolls on her back.
   d) Zac washed his hands **before** eating his sandwich.
   e) Dad drank his cup of tea **as soon as** it had cooled down.

Challenge 2
1. Sam packed his backpack with snacks, a water bottle and his favourite binoculars **before** heading to the zoo. **Then** he hopped into the car with his parents, excitedly chatting about the animals he wanted to see. **Next**, they arrived at the zoo's entrance where he eagerly handed over the tickets. They decided to visit the lions **after** visiting the ape enclosure. Sam stopped **during** their walk to watch the playful monkeys. **Soon** it was time for lunch and they strolled to the picnic area.
2. a) 4   b) 1
   c) 2   d) 5
   e) 6   f) 3

Challenge 3
1. Answers will vary. One mark for each conjunction.

Pages 24–25

Challenge 1
1. a) on   b) under
   c) in   d) over
2. a) The apple was put <u>on</u> the table.
   b) The dog hid <u>in</u> its basket.
   c) The boy climbed <u>over</u> the fence.
   d) The presents were put <u>under</u> the Christmas tree.

Challenge 2

1.
   a) The train rushed **through** the tunnel.
   b) The sun set **above** the mountains.
   c) The children had a picnic **by** the river.
   d) **Beneath** the tree was a pile of leaves.
2. under, over, beneath, above, through ✓

Challenge 3

1.
t	h	r	o	u	g	h
b	b	a	w	t	h	o
e	e	i	i	n	s	v
n	l	a	b	o	v	e
e	o	t	h	r	o	r
a	s	u	n	d	e	r
t	w	i	t	h	i	n
h	b	e	l	o	w	n

2. Yesterday, Ben went <u>on</u> a train. The journey was spectacular. The train went <u>through</u> lots of tunnels and even went <u>over</u> a bridge. Ben enjoyed looking <u>out</u> of the window at all of the beautiful scenery. He watched the sun rise high <u>in</u> the sky, <u>above</u> a castle, and he watched the waves of the sea <u>below</u> the train track.

Pages 26–27

Challenge 1

1. Answers may vary, e.g.
   a) **a** cup
   b) **an** aeroplane/**a** plane
   c) **an** elephant
   d) **a** giraffe
   e) **an** egg
   f) **a** spoon
2.
   a) **a** banana
   b) **a** shoe
   c) **an** orange

Challenge 2

1.
   a) **a** yellow bus
   b) **an** open window
   c) **a** giant octopus
   d) **an** immense hippopotamus
   e) **a** fantastic achievement
2.
   a) Yesterday, I went to **a** beach.
   b) For my lunch, I ate **an** apple.
   c) For my birthday, I got **an** amazing present.
   d) **An** octopus has eight legs.
   e) She went on **a** train.

Challenge 3

1. Answers will vary.

2. During my visit to the zoo, I saw lots of animals. My favourite was **an** Arctic polar bear. It was huge and had **a** massive jaw. It spent most of its time sleeping in **a** cave but occasionally it swam around in **a** pool. For its dinner it was fed **an** enormous fish, which it gobbled up in one go. I also loved seeing the elephants. One was **a** baby elephant. It had **an** extraordinary trunk. It looked far too big for its body!

Pages 28–29

Challenge 1

1. April, Sunday, Portugal, Mr Wood, Ethan
2. Last **Tuesday**, **I** moved to a new house on **West Road**. I share a room with my little brother **James**. You can see **Wembley Stadium** from the window. In **June**, we're going to see the **England** team play **Wales**.

Challenge 2

1.
   a) When **I** was twelve, **I** visited **London**.
   b) Bill and **Jenny** went on holiday to **Spain** in **September**.

Challenge 3

1. **Dear Mrs Porter**,

   I am having a lovely weekend in **France**. **I** arrived on **Thursday** and am not back until **August**. **Yesterday** we went shopping. **Mum** says it's going to rain tomorrow.

   See you soon.

   Mrs Porter

   Milford School

2. Answers will vary.

Pages 30–31

Challenge 1

1. At the shop, we need to buy: 1 pack of bacon, 6 eggs, 4 sausages, 2 tins of beans and 1 loaf of bread. (Items can be in any order.)

Challenge 2

1.
   a) The girl had long**,** curly**,** golden hair.
   b) It was a cold**,** grey**,** drizzly morning.
   c) The fire was blue**,** orange and red.
   d) The wood was damp**,** dark and mysterious.
   e) His eyes were blue**,** piercing and trustworthy.
   f) The petals were colourful**,** soft and scented.
2.
   a) From the market, Zayn bought three bananas, a bunch of grapes and some ham.
   b) The recipe needed two eggs, plain flour and sugar.

c) Ben tidied up his toy cars, his train track, his art set and his dominoes.
d) In Sam's money box, he had some pound coins, twenty pence pieces, five pence pieces and pennies.
e) In the baby's cot there was a rattle, a dummy and a soft toy.
f) Last night I ate a pie, some chips and a pudding.

Challenge 3

1. Bobby had to go to the shop with his mum. He wouldn't have minded but the shop was cold, boring and a long way away. The shopping list was not very long, so on the way they decided to stop at the park. He went on the swings, the slide and the roundabout. The walk to the shop was quite interesting, especially as he saw three of his friends, a really cute dog and a rabbit running across the field. When they finally got to the shop, they bought the items quickly. They got oranges, apples, bananas and kiwi fruits. They also bought some carrots, green beans and tomatoes. On the way home, he was hungry and decided to try one of the apples. It was sweet, juicy and crispy. It tasted delicious!

Pages 32–33

Challenge 1

1. wasn't ——— was not
   can't ——— cannot
   won't ——— will not
   I'll ——— I will
   wouldn't ——— would not

2. a) it's   b) he's
   c) they're   d) we've
   e) shouldn't f) isn't

Challenge 2

1.

w	'	a	t	h	n	t	s
s	w	w	a	s	n	'	t
s	a	e	'	e	h	n	'
h	e	'	l	l	t	d	n
d	f	v	h	'	s	l	a
a	w	e	t	n	e	u	c
r	'	o	'	n	g	o	'
l	'	t	r	v	m	c	s
w	o	u	l	d	n	'	t

Challenge 3

1. I love going to the cinema! **I've** been excited about seeing this film for weeks! I hope I **don't** forget to bring my ticket. **I'll** get some popcorn and a drink before it starts. You **shouldn't** talk during the film because **it's** important to let everyone enjoy it. Wow, **I didn't** realise the film was so long!

2. Answers will vary.

Pages 34–35

Challenge 1

1. a) boy's   b) cat's
   c) girl's   d) sheep's
   e) rabbit's

2. a) The **girl's** dress was torn.
   b) The **sheep's** field was extremely muddy.
   c) The **boy's** hat got blown away in the wind.
   d) The **cat's** tail became trapped in the door.
   e) The **rabbit's** burrow was invaded by ants.

Challenge 2

1. b) The <u>pupils'</u> school was closed because of the snow.
   c) The <u>trees'</u> branches waved in the wind.
   d) The <u>boys'</u> trainers were filthy.

2. b) plural   c) plural   d) singular

Challenge 3

1. a) The shop's window was broken.
   b) The boys' trousers were muddy from playing football.
   c) I went in my mum's new car.

2. I went to the **boy's** house after school today. I got to go in his **mum's** new car. It was funny because I accidentally stood in the **dog's** water bowl and my foot was soaking wet. I also played with his **brother's / brothers'** toys. Afterwards, we went in the garden. All of the **tree's / trees'** leaves had fallen off and we stamped our feet through them on the ground.

Pages 36–37

Challenge 1

1. b) "That's fantastic news."
   c) "I had a brilliant weekend."
   d) "Sit down everyone!"

2. a) "Stop that!" shouted Jacob.
   b) "I was so frightened," explained Maya to her best friend.
   c) "Why didn't you tell me before?" asked Mum.

d) "If only you knew the full story," Rory whispered.

e) "I've lost my pencil," Bessie told the teacher.

3. a) "Remember not to go near the bonfire," Dad warned.

b) "It's my birthday soon," Sebastian said excitedly.

c) "Don't be too late back," Grandpa called.

d) "Friday is my favourite day of the week," Amin told Owen.

e) "I don't like peas!" shouted Carlos.

Challenge 2

1. a) Blake said, "I love going fishing." ✓

e) "Please be careful," warned Mum. "It's very dangerous." ✓

2. a) "Today is going to be so much fun," yelled Panjit.

b) Lily whispered, "Has it gone yet?"

c) "I'm not sure about this at all!" moaned Ed.

d) "I love swimming," explained Belinda. "I'm quite good at it too!"

e) "I'm tired," said Hamish. "At least we can rest when we get home."

Challenge 3

1. "Is it nearly time to go?" asked Horace.

"I hope so," replied Alfie. "I'm so excited."

"I think it will be even better than we think!" shrieked Horace.

2. "When I get home I'm going to have a big drink of water," said Megan. "I'm very thirsty!"

"It's been a great day but I'm exhausted now," Bethan replied.

"Shall we go again tomorrow?" Megan asked.

"Definitely!" shouted Bethan.

Pages 38–41

Progress test 1

1. a) The tall tree **leaned** to the right.

b) The girl **shouted** to her friend.

c) Patrick **rode** his bike to school.

d) I **went** to the cinema.

e) The sun **slipped** behind the mountains.

2. a) There was a bowl of fruit <u>on</u> the table.

b) A wolf howled <u>beneath</u> the full moon.

c) <u>Above</u> the crowds of people, the planes flew noisily.

d) The actor waited patiently <u>behind</u> the curtain.

3. a) you're   b) I'm
c) they're   d) aren't
e) she'll

4. Dinosaur eggs often had **an** oval shape and **an** unusual texture on their shell. They could be as small as **an** orange or as big as **a** watermelon! Can you imagine finding **an** amazing egg like that? Today, you might see one in **a** museum.

5. a) I need a loaf of bread**,** a tomato and some cheese.

b) My cousin likes football, tennis, netball and swimming.

c) There was a roundabout, a burger stall, a coconut shy and a ghost train at the funfair.

d) Mum and Dad bought pizza, doughnuts, cakes**,** sweets and jelly for the party.

6. a) Charlie felt really tired **because** he went to bed late last night.

b) I wanted an ice cream **so** I asked my mum politely.

c) **When** I saw a spider, it made me jump.

d) "I will be proud **if** you try your best," said Mrs Wigley.

7. a) "I want my dinner," cried Billy.

b) The teacher asked, "Where is your homework?"

c) "Take your medicine every morning," said the kind doctor.

d) "Did you see the train?" asked Stanley, "It was fantastic."

8. a) The **boy's** tooth fell out.

b) The hamster bit the **girl's** finger.

c) **Mum's** glasses smashed into pieces on the floor.

e) The cheeky cat drank **Mary's** tea.

9. a) The snowflakes **have** fallen and covered the lawn.

b) John **has** enjoyed painting since he was young.

c) All the children **have** eaten their fruit.

d) One robin **has** visited the bird feeder.

10. then, before, soon, next, when, after

11. a) The **cows'** milk was taken to the shop to be sold.

b) The **horses'** stables were cleaned out.

c) Every day, I collect the **chickens'** eggs.

12. Commons nouns: house, star, apple, walking stick
    Proper nouns: Australia, Martha, January, The Lion King
13. a) Emily said <u>she</u> would help <u>her</u> brother with <u>his</u> homework because <u>he</u> was struggling.
    b) Liam and Sarah took **their** dog for a walk, and then **they** played with **it** in the garden.

Pages 42–43
Challenge 1
1. un — **clear**
   in — **appropriate**
   dis — **advantage**
   mis — **lead**

2. a) imperfect = **im** + **perfect**
   illogical = **il** + **logical**
   irresistible = **ir** + **resistible**
   irregular = **ir** + **regular**
   impossible = **im** + **possible**
   illegal = **il** + **legal**

3. re — **again**
   auto — **by itself**
   anti — **against**

Challenge 2
1. Answers will vary.
   a) not finished   b) read incorrectly
   c) don't obey   d) not convenient

Challenge 3
1. Answers will vary.

Pages 44–45
Challenge 1
1. <u>anti</u>clockwise — moving in the opposite direction to the way the hands on a clock move
   <u>auto</u>matic — working by itself with little or no direct human control
   <u>re</u>write — to write something again

Challenge 2
1.
Prefix	Root word
mis	**take**
un	**comfortable**
ir	**rational**
anti	**gravity**
auto	**graph**

Challenge 3
1. a) Tottenham's goal was **disallowed** because it was offside.
   b) At a party, I was **reintroduced** to someone I had met before.
   c) I was given **antibiotics** to fight off my illness.
   d) We bought an **automatic** car.
   e) Breaking a glass is **irreversible** because you can't put it back together again.
   f) Naomi **misunderstood** the instructions and went to the wrong classroom.

2. The school trip to the zoo was almost ruined by the **unexpected** rain. It was **impossible** to see the animals through the fogged-up windows of the bus. Some of the children felt it was **disappointing**, especially since the trip had been planned for months. We had to leave early which meant the children's work was **incomplete**. Hopefully, the teacher will be able to **reschedule** the trip.

Pages 46–47
Challenge 1
1. a) proudly   b) suddenly
   c) strangely d) peacefully
2. Answers will vary.

Challenge 2
1. happy — happily; angry — angrily; gentle — gently; simple — simply; basic — basically; dramatic — dramatically

Challenge 3
1. a) vari<u>ous</u>   b) mountain<u>ous</u>
   c) horrend<u>ous</u> d) danger<u>ous</u>
   e) poison<u>ous</u>   f) courage<u>ous</u>

2. fabulous — extraordinary or wonderful
   jealous — feeling resentment for what other people have
   obvious — easy to see, understand or recognise
   hideous — extremely unpleasant

118

3. a) serious b) enormous
   c) glorious d) joyous
   e) ridiculous

Pages 48–49

Challenge 1
1. a) pic**ture** b) mea**sure**
2. a) pres**sure** b) mix**ture**
   c) clo**sure**

Challenge 2
1. a) crea**ture** b) frac**ture**
   c) sculp**ture** d) furni**ture**
   e) enclo**sure** f) lei**sure**
2. a) The fearsome **creature** was guarding the **treasure** in the cave.
   b) My favourite **pleasure** in life is to walk among **nature**.

Challenge 3
1. Answers will vary.

Pages 50–51

Challenge 1
1. a) searching ——— **search**
   b) dropped ——— **drop**
   c) disagree ——— **agree**
   d) replay ——— **play**
2. Answers will vary, e.g.
   b) jump + ed = **jumped**
   c) high + er = **higher**
   d) low + est = **lowest**
   e) brilliant + ly = **brilliantly**

Challenge 2
1.
Root word	Prefix	New word
b) behave	mis	misbehave
c) way	sub	subway
d) correct	in	incorrect

2.
Root word	Prefix	New word
b) danger	ous	dangerous
c) amaze	ment	amazement
d) care	ful	careful

Challenge 3
1.
c	r	e	a	t	i	o	n	l	z
o	q	i	s	o	f	t	l	y	r
n	d	m	n	i	f	v	o	n	e
f	o	u	r	t	z	q	j	e	d
u	f	a	s	t	e	s	t	h	i
s	l	l	h	a	g	r	d	o	r
i	b	c	p	e	f	t	a	n	e
o	e	t	w	i	y	z	k	c	c
n	a	u	t	o	p	i	l	o	t

confusion, interact, softly, redirect, creation, autopilot

Pages 52–53

Challenge 1
1.
Root word	+	Suffix	New word
b) fit	+	ing	**fitting**
c) prefer	+	ed	**preferred**
d) begin	+	ing	**beginning**

2. a) slipping
   b) jumped
   c) sitting

Challenge 2
1.
Root word	Suffix	New word
a) clap	ing	clapping
travel	er	b) traveller
c) spot	d) ed	spotted
stop	ed	e) stopped
begin	er	f) beginner

Challenge 3
1. Answers will vary.
2. Answers will vary.

Pages 54–55

Challenge 1
1. echo ——— a repeating sound
   character ——— a person in a book, film or play
   chemist ——— a person or place you can buy medicine from

Challenge 2

1. ma**ch**ine ✓
   bro**ch**ure ✓
   mousta**ch**e ✓
   chute ✓

2. a) 'c' is silent
   b) science ———— Latin (**s** sound)
   chorus ———— Greek (**k** sound)
   para**ch**ute ———— French (**sh** sound)

Challenge 3

1.
	g	k
a) league	✓	
b) cheque		✓
c) antique		✓
d) vague	✓	

Pages 56–57

Challenge 1

1. misplace ———— to lose something
   illegal ———— not legal
   disappear ———— vanish from view
   irregular ———— not regular

2. a) disagree ———— **not agree**
   b) unchanged ———— **not changed**
   c) misunderstand ———— **not understand**

Challenge 2

1. a) not finished b) not sure c) pain
2. disable, unfriendly, mismatch, incapable

Challenge 3

1. Answers will vary but should include the following meanings:
   a) not patient
   b) to spell wrongly
   c) not to obey

Pages 58–59

Challenge 1

1. a) sea b) male c) sun
   d) be e) won f) grown
   g) blew h) to / too

Challenge 2

1. berry ———— a small, juicy fruit
   bury ———— to put in the ground and cover with earth
   ball ———— a sphere
   bawl ———— to shout out
   medal ———— an award for bravery or winning a race
   meddle ———— to interfere with something

Challenge 3

1. a) The blister on my **heel** took some time to **heal**.
   b) We **missed** our turning because the road sign was hidden by the **mist**.
   c) Mum uses the **brake** when she is driving to make sure she does not **break** the speed limit.
   d) I could **not** undo the **knot** in my shoelace.
   e) When we had **seen** the last **scene** of the play, everyone clapped.

2. Answers will vary.

Pages 60–61

Challenge 1

1. a) because b) fruit c) February
   d) surprise e) busy f) imagine
   g) caught h) through

2. happened, bought, come, once, where, bicycle

Challenge 2

1. Correct spelling: decided, started, getting, answer
   Incorrect spelling: frightend, anuther, thort, famus
   Corrected spelling: frightened, another, thought, famous

Challenge 3

1. Sophie couldn't **believe** it was **Monday** again. "I **always** wish the weekend was longer," she **said** with a sigh. "I **can't** wait to do **something** fun."

2. Answers will vary. Check for correct spelling.

Pages 62–63

Challenge 1

1. a, e, i, o, u
2. b, c, d, f, g, h, j, k, l, m, n, p, q, r, s, t, v, w, x, y, z
   (5 marks for all consonants correctly circled with no vowels. Deduct 1 mark for each incorrect vowel.)

Challenge 2

1. Only award 5 marks if the correct pattern has been followed. There are no marks for getting this partly correct.

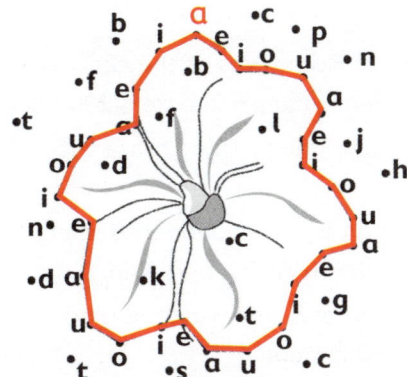

2. 5 marks for all vowels correctly joined in order. Deduct 1 mark for each consonant.

Challenge 3

1. a) t b) u c) s d) a
2. a — A, e — E, i — I, o — O, u — U
3. B C D F G H J
   K L M N P Q R
   S T V W X Y Z

Pages 64–65

Challenge 1

1. a) angrily b) mixture
   c) orange d) unkind
   e) usually
2. Answers will vary.
3. Answers will vary.

Challenge 2

1. gardening, prefer, begin, limited
2. finaly — finally, missbehave — misbehave, informacion — information

Challenge 3

1. Have you ever wished you could make your chores **dissapear** with just a snap of your fingers? That would **probally** be everyone's **favrit** trick! But instead, we can **lurn** how to make them fun. For example, try turning cleaning your room into a race to see how much you can tidy in just one **minit**. Soon **enuff**, you might find yourself laughing as you put toys away, and before you know it, everything is done!

   a) disappear b) probably
   c) favourite d) learn
   e) minute f) enough

Pages 66–67

Challenge 1

1. **nocturnal** — active at night
   hexagon — a 2-D shape with six straight sides
   easel — an upright frame to hold a picture that someone is painting
   autobiography — a book about a person's own life
   abundance — a large amount of something
   colossal — extremely large

Challenge 2

1. Answers will vary, depending on dictionary used.

Challenge 3

1. Answers will vary.
2. Answers will vary, depending on dictionary used.

Pages 68–71

Progress test 2

1. a) fair b) great c) plain
   d) bare e) main f) night
   g) meet h) rain / rein

2.

s	m	o	s	k	v	u	r
t	s	c	h	o	o	l	k
o	j	c	x	d	e	a	b
m	c	d	e	z	l	m	z
a	x	t	o	n	g	u	e
c	h	a	l	e	t	s	i
h	u	r	q	o	o	c	g
w	e	e	f	y	t	l	p
i	m	o	s	q	u	e	n

3. a) grabbed   b) swimming
    c) regretted   d) dripping
4. a) **mis**understood b) **un**happy
    c) **dis**honest   d) **in**complete
5. 0 vowels: cry, rhythm
    1 vowel: kind, tick, fork
    2 vowels: open, some, apple
6. hideous, nervous, gracious
7. Answers will vary.
8. a) can't   b) don't   c) won't
9. a) **im**patient   b) **il**legal
    c) **im**mature   d) **il**legible
    e) **im**possible
10. Answers will vary.
11. Answers will vary, depending on dictionary used.
12. The flowers grew because Betty had watered them. — **conjunction**
    I closed the door quietly behind me. — **adverb**
    Arthur put the letters through the letter box. — **preposition**
    April is the rainiest month. — **proper noun**

Pages 72–73

Challenge 1
1. a) **Approximately** 2000 years ago, Rome was at the centre of the Roman Empire.
    b) This Empire ruled **more than 45 million people**.
    c) Its army was the most **powerful** in the world.
    d) It conquered many parts of **Europe, North Africa** and Asia.
    e) More than **a million** people lived in Rome.
    f) Rome was a **bustling** place.
    g) People living in Rome attended **gladiator** fights.
    h) Rome was also dirty and **dangerous**.

Challenge 2
1. a) The city of Rome was at the centre of the Roman Empire approximately 2000 years ago.
    b) The Roman Empire ruled more than 45 million people.
    c) The Roman Empire conquered many parts of Europe, North Africa and Asia.
    d) The people of Rome watched gladiators fight for entertainment.

Challenge 3
1. powerful — strong, hard to defeat
    approximately — about
    attending — going to
    conquered — overcame and took control
    bustling — busy, lively

Pages 74–75

Challenge 1
1. a) The well was very **deep**.
    b) She had plenty of **time** as she went down.
    c) First, she tried to **look down**.
    d) But it was too **dark** to see anything.
    e) She took a jar that was labelled **orange marmalade** but to her disappointment it was empty.

Challenge 2
1. a) three
    b) glass
    c) a tiny golden key
    d) the key might belong to one of the doors
    e) about fifteen inches high

Challenge 3
1. a) small and dark
    b) not much larger than a rat-hole
    c) How she longed to get out of that dark hall.
    d) she could not even get her head through the doorway

Pages 76–77

Challenge 1
1. a) *Little Red Riding Hood*
    b) *Cinderella*
    c) *Jack and the Beanstalk*

Challenge 2

1.

Traditional tale	Hero / Heroine	Villain(s)
a) *Jack and the Beanstalk*	Jack	Giant
b) *Cinderella*	Cinderella	Ugly Sisters
c) *The Three Little Pigs*	The third pig	Wolf
d) *Little Red Riding Hood*	Woodcutter	Wolf
e) *Hansel and Gretel*	Hansel and Gretel	Witch

Challenge 3

1. Answers may be extended but basic answers should include:
   a) Wood, Grandma's house
   b) Little Red Riding Hood, Woodcutter, Grandma
   c) Wolf
   d) Wolf eats Grandma.
   e) Woodcutter saves the day.
   f) Wolf is killed / made harmless.

Pages 78–79

Challenge 1

1. wolf, wicked stepmother, fairy godmother, princess
2. a) Fairy Godmother — **magical**
   b) Big Bad Wolf — **cunning**
   c) Princess — **kind-hearted**
   d) Woodcutter — **brave**
   e) Ugly Sister — **selfish**

Challenge 2

1. **Heroes / Heroines**: strong, courageous, caring, kind, generous
   Villains: rude, untrustworthy, greedy, dishonest, sly
2. Answers will vary, e.g. for princess: beautiful, generous, kind, caring, rich; for troll: scary, menacing, ugly, evil, huge.

Challenge 3

1. a) good
   b) Answers will vary, e.g. charming, kind, smile, generous, gave money and food to the poor, took care of her sick aunt.

Pages 80–81

Challenge 1

1. a) **Everyone** grumbled. The sky was grey.
   b) And everyone's face grew **merry** and **bright**.
   c) "He's crawling out of the **duckweed**!"
2. Answers will vary. Examples:
   a) bright and delight
   b) say and day

Challenge 2

1. Answers will vary. Examples:
   a) complained   b) poor
   c) happy   d) giggled
2. a) Click!
   b) Daddy fell into the pond!

Challenge 3

1. Answers will vary. Examples:
   a) A son because he thinks it's funny that Daddy fell into the pond.
   b) He is trying not to laugh.
   c) Happy because it was funny.

Pages 82–83

Challenge 1

1.

	Fact	Description
a) The sun shone brightly in the sky like an orange ball.		✓
b) I went bowling yesterday.	✓	
c) About 1 in 10 people are vegetarian.	✓	
d) She meandered through the crowds like a snake stalking its prey.		✓

2. a) Come to Zak's fun fair. You'll have the time of your life! — **to persuade**
   b) The supermarket opens daily from 7am until 10pm. — **to inform**
   c) With a hood covering his face, a mysterious figure emerged from the dark shadows. — **to entertain**

Challenge 2

1.
   a) to inform
   b) to persuade
   c) to entertain
   d) to inform
   e) to entertain
   f) to persuade

Challenge 3

1.
   a) The purpose of the advert is to get people to book a trip into space.
   b) The writer has used the phrase 'once-in-a-lifetime' because people will only be able to go once. This may be because of cost.
   c) The writer has started the advert with a question to draw the reader in / get the reader's attention.
   d) The writer has used the phrase 'out of this world' because the trip will be into space (and also a 'once-in-a-lifetime' opportunity).

Pages 84–85

Challenge 1

1. Arya tastes the mixture to check if it's sweet enough.

   Kian might remember seeing her add the sugar earlier.

   Arya decides to add the sugar anyway, just in case.

Challenge 2

1.
   a) Answers will vary, e.g. It started to rain and they had to go home.
   b) Answers will vary, e.g. She crashed her car.

Challenge 3

1. Answers will vary. Two marks should be awarded for a prediction, e.g. I think she will go and get an ice cream from the ice-cream van, even though she knows she might get into trouble.

Pages 86–87

Challenge 1

1.
   a) morning
   b) It is light outside.
   c) four
   d) There are four glasses.

Challenge 2

1.
   a) sad / unhappy
   b) happy
   c) surprised / shocked

Challenge 3

1.
   a) Alyssa <u>sat</u> in the corner, tears <u>rolling</u> down her face.
   b) Jemma's face <u>turned</u> redder and redder as she <u>clenched</u> her fists together.
   c) <u>Jumping</u> up and down, Jonah <u>giggled</u> with glee.
   d) Aaron <u>ripped</u> his work into lots of pieces and <u>marched</u> out of the room.
   e) With his arms <u>folded</u>, a scowl <u>crossed</u> the headteacher's face.

2. Answers will vary e.g.
   a) Alyssa **was sad**.
   b) Jemma **was angry**.
   c) Jonah **was happy**.
   d) Aaron **was frustrated.**
   e) The headteacher **was disappointed**.

Pages 88–89

Challenge 1

1.
   a) morning
   b) too cold
   c) drink something

Challenge 2

1.
   a) The street was <u>bustling</u> with lots of tourists. — **busy**
   b) Darkness <u>engulfed</u> the town, hiding it from view. — **covered completely**
   c) The boys were <u>ravenous</u>. They hadn't eaten since lunchtime. — **hungry**
   d) The cars were <u>stationary</u> in a traffic jam. — **not moving**

2.
   a) Around him, almost everyone **had shorts on**.
   b) The **sun sizzled** in the sky.
   c) Puddles that had been there before had now **dried up**.

Challenge 3

1. <u>Crowds packed</u> the streets. There were <u>tourists everywhere</u>. Every shop was <u>crowded</u> and there was <u>barely space for anyone to fit through the doors</u>. Visitors meandered, slowly moving across the square. They <u>added to the volume of people</u> in

the streets and created a <u>human traffic jam</u>. There was no shelter from the sun today. <u>Every inch of shade was occupied</u>.

Pages 90–93

Progress test 3

1. *Little Red Riding Hood, Hansel and Gretel, Jack and the Beanstalk*
2. Answers will vary.
3. a) serious   b) possible   c) decide
4. a) fiction
   b) Peter
   c) was put in a pie by Mrs McGregor
   d) blackberries
   e) lettuces, French beans
5. verb — planting
   common noun — cucumber
   proper noun — Mopsy
   preposition — underneath
6. a) Peter met Mr McGregor round the end of a cucumber frame.
   b) Mr McGregor shouted, "Stop thief." at Peter.
   c) Answers will vary. E.g. Mr McGregor felt angry when he saw Peter.
   d) Peter felt frightened when he could not remember the way back to the gate.
7. Answers will vary.
8. Answers will vary.
9. a) "Now, my dears," said old Mrs Rabbit.
   b) Mr McGregor called out, "Stop thief!"

Pages 94–95

Challenge 1
1. a) verb   b) adjective
   c) noun   d) verb
   e) noun

Challenge 2
1. a) The **enormous** tree towered over the forest.
   b) Three of the **naughty** puppies chewed up the man's slipper.
   c) The **beautiful** woman was sitting quietly by the waterfall.
   d) Behind the **empty** park was a **huge** field.
   e) Jane took her **new** fish tank home and put it in her bedroom.
   f) The sky was **dark**, **black** and **stormy**.
2. a)–e)   Answers will vary.

Challenge 3
1. a)–c)   Answers will vary.
2. Answers will vary.

Pages 96–97

Challenge 1
1. She ran towards the door. ✓ It swayed. ✓ There was silence. ✓
2.

	Sentence	Phrase
a) The bird soared high in the sky.	✓	
b) Quietly, the rabbit retreated.	✓	
c) From the darkness		✓
d) It emerged.	✓	
e) Above the trees		✓

Challenge 2
1. because I was hungry — **a clause**
   to the swimming pool — **a phrase**
   My house is in London. — **a statement**
   How many pizzas do we need? — **a question**
   Wow, a hot air balloon! — **an exclamation**
   that sweet little mouse — **a noun phrase**

Challenge 3
1. Answers may vary, e.g.
   a) Out of the darkness, **a light suddenly appeared.**
   b) As the sun began to set, **they headed for home.**
   c) When the bell rang, **the teacher ended the lesson.**
   d) From behind the tree, **a mysterious figure emerged.**
   e) With a smile on his face, **he unwrapped the gift.**
2. Answers will vary.

Pages 98–99

Challenge 1

1. a) **On Monday,** ——— I started a new week at school.
   b) **When my alarm went off,** ——— I jumped out of bed.
   c) **Before lunch,** ——— I washed my hands.
   d) **After Art class,** ——— I got my things for home time.
   e) **At 8 o'clock in the evening,** ——— I went to bed.

2. a) During the night**,** the owls left their nests to hunt.
   b) Aged four**,** I went on my first holiday abroad.
   c) On Tuesdays**,** I have my saxophone lesson at school.
   d) At 3.15 pm**,** the bell rang to go home.
   e) After my bath**,** I got ready for bed.

Challenge 2

1. a) After **breakfast**, I brushed my teeth.
   b) At **12 o'clock**, I ate my lunch.
   c) Before **sunset / sunrise**, I returned home.
   d) On **Saturday**, I played football.

2. a) <u>After dinner</u>, I played on the computer.
   b) <u>In an instant</u>, the wood fell quiet.
   c) <u>With the saddle on her horse</u>, Lucy was ready to go riding.

Challenge 3

1. Answers will vary, e.g.
   a) <u>As soon as it started to rain</u>, I quickly ran inside.
   b) <u>After lunch</u>, I have PE at school.
   c) <u>On hearing my alarm</u>, I woke up.
   d) <u>On Saturday</u>, I will go on holiday.

Pages 100–101

Challenge 1

1. Introduction ——— What a robin is and what the report will tell the reader
   Appearance ——— What a robin looks like
   Diet ——— What a robin eats
   Habitat ——— Where a robin lives
   Conclusion ——— A summary of the main points

Challenge 2

1. Answers will vary, e.g. Introduction, What is a guinea pig?

Challenge 3

1. Answers will vary.
2. Answers will vary.

Pages 102–103

Challenge 1

1. a) Beginning   b) Middle   c) End

2. a) **Beginning** ——— The setting and the main characters are introduced.
   b) **Middle** ——— There is a problem or something changes in the story.
   c) **End** ——— The problem is solved.

Challenge 2

1. Answers will vary.
2. Answers will vary.

Challenge 3

1. Answers will vary.

Pages 104–105

Challenge 1

1. Answers will vary (1 mark for each bullet point).

Challenge 2

1. Answers will vary (1 mark for each correct adjective).

Challenge 3

1. Answers will vary (1 mark for each interesting idea and adjective, maximum 5 marks).

Pages 106–107

Challenge 1

1. a) The road was wet <u>becouse</u> it had been raining. **because**
   b) Ivan and Ella helped to <u>billed</u> the model. **build**
   c) The bird <u>wos</u> flying through the air. **was**

2.
	Punctuation	Spelling
b) <u>Ive</u> read all of the books on my shelf.	✗	✓
c) The cat ran <u>threw</u> the open window.	✓	✗
d) Mei saw <u>birds</u> fish and snakes in the pet shop	✗	✓
e) I <u>couldnt</u> carry the <u>heavey</u> shopping.	✗	✗

Challenge 2

1.
	,	.	,
a) The school holidays last for seven **weeks.**		✓	
b) We ate **peas,** carrots and potatoes for lunch.			✓
c) Our dog Alvin **didn't** want to go for a walk.	✓		
d) **We've** been waiting a long time for the **bus.**	✓	✓	

2. a) **Anil** didn't want to go to the cinema on **Monday.**
   b) **The** family went to **Paris** on their holidays.
   c) **The** rain in **January** was worse than in **December.**
   d) **Elijah** and **Chantal couldn't** find their car keys in the house.

Challenge 3

1. **Smudge** was a **naughty** little puppy who loved getting into trouble. One day, he **wouldn't** stop digging in **Dad's** garden, even though he was told not to. Smudge **thought** it was the perfect place to hide his favourite bone, but when Dad saw the mess, he **wasn't** happy! Smudge **tried** to look innocent, but **there** was mud, grass and daisies all over his nose and paws. **Everyone** laughed, and even Dad had to smile – **Smudge always** found a way to make things fun.

Pages 108–111

Progress test 4

1. a) Egyptians built pyramids for their kings. ✓
   b) Much of Egypt is desert. ✓
   e) The capital of Egypt is Cairo. ✓

2. a) They **were** happy.
   b) **Mum didn't** like my **favourite** rollercoaster ride.
   c) On **Tuesdays,** we go to karate.
   d) James and **Bill** are coming to the park. They are coming in **Dad's** car.
   e) Jill **has** danced in five shows in **February.**

3. a) The <u>green</u> grass danced in the wind.
   b) The <u>dark</u> forest loomed in the distance.
   c) The pirate had a <u>multi-coloured</u> parrot.
   d) She ran towards the <u>empty</u> house.
   e) I heard the <u>rusty</u> gate creak in the wind.

4. Answers will vary, e.g. long, slithery, spotty, yellow

5. Answers will vary.

6. a) **The colossal** waterfall crashed onto **the sodden** rocks.
   b) **Ten minuscule mice** scuttled past **the petrified shopkeeper.**
   c) **Their scorching** teas steamed in **the icy air.**

7. Answers will vary.

8. Answers will vary.

9. a) quietly   b) safely
   c) rapidly   d) suddenly

10. Answers will vary, e.g.
    The ~~tall~~ towering walls of the ancient castle loomed overhead as Leo ~~walked~~ stumbled cautiously across the crumbling stone bridge, the wind ~~blowing~~ whistling around him. He ran his fingers over the ~~gold~~ shiny medallion in his pocket. He had to return it to the ~~good~~ magnificent king. Suddenly, a loud clang echoed behind him, and he jumped, ~~turning~~ spinning around to see the rusty portcullis slamming shut. He ~~looked~~ stared up towards the battlements and froze. A ~~dark~~ spooky figure stood there, pointing directly at him. Before he could decide whether to ~~run~~ sprint away or hide, the ground beneath him began to shake.

11. Answers will vary.

Progress test charts

Use these charts to record your results in the four Progress tests. Colour in the questions that you got right to help you identify any areas that you might need to study and practise again. (These areas are indicated in the 'See page…' row in the charts.)

Progress test 1:

	Q1	Q2	Q3	Q4	Q5	Q6	Q7	Q8	Q9	Q10	Q11	Q12	Q13	TOTAL /68
See page…	14–15	24–25	32–33	26–27	30–31	20–21	36–37	34–35	16–17	22–23	34–35	12–13	12–13	

Progress test 2:

	Q1	Q2	Q3	Q4	Q5	Q6	Q7	Q8	Q9	Q10	Q11	Q12	TOTAL /57
See page…	58–59	54–55	52–53	42–45	62–63	46–47	64–65	32–33	42–45	14–15	66–67	12–25	

Progress test 3:

	Q1	Q2	Q3	Q4	Q5	Q6	Q7	Q8	Q9	TOTAL /27
See page…	76–79	64–67	60–61	72–75	12–25	72–75	84–85	82–83	36–37	

Progress test 4:

	Q1	Q2	Q3	Q4	Q5	Q6	Q7	Q8	Q9	Q10	Q11	TOTAL /67
See page…	100–101	106–107	94–95	104–105	104–105	94–95	96–97	98–99	46–47	94–95	102–103	

What am I doing well in?

....

....

....

What do I need to improve?

....

....

....